"Adrien and his wife, Stacey, exempl[...] they do, both individually and togeth[...] boys to pursuing their own unique endeavours, they create an environment of acceptance, love, encouragement, and perseverance that everyone around them can feel as soon as they enter their presence. Specifically, we have been honoured to witness Adrien's commitment to growth throughout the past several years, including his ability to focus on his goals and continuing to strive for them despite hardships and frustration. His optimism, passion, and zeal for life are endless. Even when he faces difficulty, he does so with an undertone of gratitude for the people and opportunities he has in his life. We should all be so blessed to have people like Adrien and Stacey in our lives."

—Taylor and Nicole Breckenridge
Directors, C2C Leadership Inc., Entrepreneurs, International Speakers

"You can't know Adrien and his wife Stacey without first watching their family at Sunday Dinner. The whole house is alive with chatter. Loved ones, young, old, and in between, are congregating to commune together. There is a sense of relaxed chaos. Chaos that evolves to calm a satiation when everyone has had their fill. Their children are open, gregarious, and polite, full of questions and eager to learn from every conversation. Adrien and Stacey have already accomplished what so many can only dream of in their family environment. Adrien, through his calm, caring demeanour, creates a welcoming, open presence that can and will grace anyone he comes into contact with. If he sets a goal, I have no doubt that he would carry it out in the most articulate and well-thought-out manner. Anyone who is fortunate enough to be involved in the achieving of that goal can rest assured that they are in good hands."

—Gwen Seal
Past Regional Director Heart Stone Group

*"Humans have communicated with each other since the beginning of time. Verbal communication was one of the earliest forms. One of the most efficient and engrossing types of verbal communication was through storytelling. Stories, principally life stories, can help us make sense of our purpose in this world. It can teach us life lessons and help us cope with perplexing situations. It can promote relationships and empathy, and with it, the improvement of self and society. Mr. Adrian has intriguingly and delightfully shared his life story in his book. Being a devout Catholic and belonging to St. Maria Goretti parish, it is indubitably a splendid feeling that he has brought forward a motivating book, which as the parish priest, I would recommend for everyone's reading."*

—Fr. Arun Rodrigues SAC
Pastor, St. Maria Goretti Catholic Church

# JOURNEY TO SUCCESS

## with **ADRIEN FOUILLARD**

ALSO FEATURING
OTHER TOP AUTHORS

© 2021 Success Publishing

Success Publishing, LLC
P.O. Box 703536
Dallas, Texas 75370 USA

questions@mattmorris.com

All rights reserved. No part of this book may be reproduced, stored in a retrieval system, or transmitted in any form or by any means - electronic or mechanical, photocopy, recording, or any other - except for brief quotations in printed reviews, without the prior permission of the publisher. Although the author(s) and publisher have made every effort to ensure the accuracy and completeness of information contained in this book, we assume no responsibility for errors, inaccuracies, omissions, or any inconsistency herein.

# Table of Contents

1. Shaky Beginnings . . . . . . . . . . . . . . . . . . . 9
   By Adrien Fouillard

2. Journey To Success . . . . . . . . . . . . . . . . . . 15
   By Matt Morris

3. Scared Shitless . . . . . . . . . . . . . . . . . . . . 23
   By Steve Moreland

4. My American Dream . . . . . . . . . . . . . . . . . 33
   By Alden Porter III

5. What Full Commitment Can Truly Do . . . . . . . . . . . 39
   By Caroline Lekanyang

6. Bullied, But Never Beaten! . . . . . . . . . . . . . . . 45
   By Cayle Lawrence

7. The Extra Mile . . . . . . . . . . . . . . . . . . . . 51
   By Chuck Spitzer

8. Battle With Fear . . . . . . . . . . . . . . . . . . . 57
   By Cyrill May Stewart

9. So, I Failed. So What?! . . . . . . . . . . . . . . . . 63
   By Deborah Clay

10. Self-Discipline Through Internal And External Focus . . . . . . 69
    By Derrick Wilson

11. The Monster In My Bed . . . . . . . . . . . . . . . 75
    By Doreen Stroud

12. Comradery Over Intimidation: Building Teams
    Because Things Can Always Be Worse . . . . . . . . . . . . . . . 83
    *By Eric Stiles*

13. Giving Up Is The Only Failure . . . . . . . . . . . . . . . . . . 91
    *By Geoff Cash*

14. The Center Of Building Your Relationship With Others . . . . . 95
    *By Henry Atchison*

15. 9G's To T-10 . . . . . . . . . . . . . . . . . . . . . . . . . . . 103
    *By Jack Thomas, Jr.*

16. The Keys To Unlocking Your Prison . . . . . . . . . . . . . . . 109
    *By Jameson Chin*

17. How You Want To Be Remembered In Life Is Up To You . . . . . 117
    *By Javi Utreras*

18. The Power To Succeed . . . . . . . . . . . . . . . . . . . . . . 123
    *By Jessica Okobia*

19. The Secret Of Your Power . . . . . . . . . . . . . . . . . . . . 131
    *By Karyne Lauret*

20. StEPs: They All Count! . . . . . . . . . . . . . . . . . . . . . 139
    *By Kaydell Barron*

21. Fat, Ugly, Queer To Fabulous And Successful
    Business Professional Mindset: Overcoming Everyday
    Obstacles, Negativity, And Self-Doubt To Create A
    Perfect New You! . . . . . . . . . . . . . . . . . . . . . . . . . 145
    *By Larry C. LeSueur*

22. The Secret Of Resurrecting Your Purpose Of Life
    Through Creating A "Dream-Board" . . . . . . . . . . . . . . . 155
    *By Lena Jo*

23. A Tale Of Love, Setbacks, And Successes . . . . . . . . . . . . . . . 161
    *By Michael Wesley*

24. Unwavering Determination And A Mother's Love . . . . . . . . 169
    *By Mwansa Palangwa Gold*

25. God's Undeniable LOVE . . . . . . . . . . . . . . . . . . . . . 177
    *By Naquita Rae Rivas*

26. A Paradoxical Paradox . . . . . . . . . . . . . . . . . . . . . 183
    *By Oluwafunmike Ani*

27. Inner Conflict . . . . . . . . . . . . . . . . . . . . . . . . . 191
    *By Shaun Bass*

28. Whatever It Takes. . . . . . . . . . . . . . . . . . . . . . . . 197
    *By Sinan Abu-Aisheh*

29. The Other Side Of Forgiveness . . . . . . . . . . . . . . . . . 205
    *By Stephanie Woodley*

30. Accounting For The Unknown . . . . . . . . . . . . . . . . . . 211
    *By Tet Dela Cruz*

31. Tragic Blessings. . . . . . . . . . . . . . . . . . . . . . . . . 217
    *By Todd and Gina Strand*

32. Everyone Can Be A Winner. . . . . . . . . . . . . . . . . . . 225
    *By Wincy Chan*

CHAPTER 1

# Shaky Beginnings

*By Adrien Fouillard*

I am just an ordinary guy. It took me fifty-three years to realize that ordinary was not going to get me ahead. I was really just a quintessential follower and people pleaser. Building a successful life was not that important to me. Pleasure-seeking and recreational activities took firm precedence.

I was fortunate to have been raised in a great family by loving parents and siblings. My parents both served people on a daily basis. They truly took their eyes off themselves and put them on others. They were the best role models ever! I am proud to share that my father was a World War II veteran, having served in the Air Force throughout the war. It was always in my subconscious to join the Canadian Forces.

At fourteen, my parents sent me 200 miles away to a Catholic school, where I boarded at a seminary. This was in hopes of getting at least one priest out of eight boys. I resented their decision and rebelled. During this period, a couple of disgraceful incidents took place: nearly overdosing on LSD and eventually getting kicked out of the seminary, just so my parents could find me a new home. Schooling was easy for me, so I was still able to graduate four years later despite all my immaturity. A couple of hurtful events followed in the next few years: one of these was the loss of a nephew and niece, whose lives were taken by cystic fibrosis at the very young age of eight. I just did not find that fair and needed to lean into my faith through those great losses.

One would think that I learned my lesson, but through the years, the pleasure-seeking, destructive patterns continued through college and various jobs. One shattering experience with an unwanted pregnancy between two irresponsible kids (my girlfriend and me) made me rethink my position in life. It was a tough lesson, but we mutually ended the relationship through decisions out of our control. I now needed to figure out my next step in life. As I reflected on my past lesson, I decided to make a second attempt to join the Canadian Navy at the age of twenty-three in 1991. My application to the Airforce in 1986, at eighteen, was rejected because of the drugs in my system at the time (a very embarrassing situation). However, this time was different; I was recruited in the Navy as a Naval Weapons Technician.

I am proud to say that I made it through basic training, winning the Platoon Achievement Award (an award for someone who sucks at everything, but I never gave up and figured it out). In the first year, en route to Halifax, while on party mode during graduation night, I was charged for driving under the influence. I lost my license for a year. As I mentioned, on my first deployment, I was fortunate to participate in a six-month peacekeeping mission in 1992. This took place in the Persian Gulf, aboard the HMCS Restigouche. I got to see a bit of the world during this voyage, being initiated from Tadpole to Shellback by crossing the Equator and crossing the International Date Line. This meant that I had started my voyage on the West Coast and completed it after a full tour around the world and ending up on the West Coast. Pretty cool!

The most important part, and the greatest thing ever about my joining the Navy, was that after this six-month voyage, at the end of September (on the 29th, to be precise), I met Stacey: the beautiful and smart woman who I would soon call my wife! Things moved pretty quickly with us. At first, I moved in with her as just a roommate. But this lasted about a week after the two of us developed feelings beyond just being roommates—if you know what I mean. This escalated, and the two of us were married on May 01, 1993, and Stacey gave birth to Christian on December 24, 1993.

Side note. If you do the math, she was already pregnant before we were married—something my mother eventually figured out.

Life started great! I loved sailing and learning the trade, but I was missing valuable time with my family. Instead, I just numbed myself with alcohol to mask the sadness. I would call my wife when I was in foreign ports, wishing the family could be with me. However, a lack of money did not allow that. As difficult as it was, I signed a second contract. I was offered a move to Halifax with my family to attend a two-year Naval Weapons Technician course at the engineering school in Stadacona.

Gratitude was not in my dictionary—not until after this scary situation! Our second son, Nathaniel, was born three and a half weeks premature due to complications with placenta abruption. Luckily, both survived, just short of fifteen minutes! It was crazy how it worked out! I am not proud to say this, but I was about a half-hour away, inebriated after having helped a friend move into a new house. When Stacey called me, I knew something was majorly wrong; she could not move off the couch and was in pain. I phoned Grace Hospital, and they informed me to get her there as quickly as I could, as they would not be able to get to her quickly enough. Just the thought of losing her and my son instantly sobered me. That is my story. It was a blur! This story is a true success, even with my poor decision of drinking and driving once again. But this time, it was for a much better reason. I got her to the hospital, with her feeling every bump and me racing through red lights and rushing through traffic. Luckily, it was evening, and traffic was pretty mild. Great turnout! The emergency was a success: mom and baby were safe. However, Nathaniel was hospitalized in an incubator for a week. Today, he is a very healthy twenty-six-year-old. As I alluded to earlier, that was truly my first real lesson about gratitude. Through these challenging situations, my faith gave me strength.

I was in fleet school, and my wife and kids were homed in military housing. We were hardly making ends meet. At times, we had to sneak some money out of the kids' piggy bank to purchase a jug of milk—a pretty sad situation, I know. We eventually figured out how to tighten our budget, and at times, we were blessed with grandma sending us care packages and treats. Sometimes, she would even slip in a fifty-dollar bill. Things always seemed to work out.

After my course graduation in Halifax, we moved back to Victoria, where I sailed for another year and a half. Because of much time at sea and not being able to prioritize time with family, both Stacey and I agreed that I would end my second naval contract in 1997 and pursue a career in hydraulics, which led us to Manitoba. Trying to impress my employer and coworkers, I embarked on a workaholic, overtime-filled journey, almost forgetting I had a wife and two kids at home. Occasionally, I would use my hard work as an excuse to go drinking. What a jerk I can be at times!

While we were in Winnipeg, I experienced the most humbling, enriching, and probably one of my saddest moments ever: the passing of my sister, Sarah. She passed away at the age of forty-one, taken by cancer while pregnant, losing her baby in the process. She was also the mother of the two children who passed away from cystic fibrosis years earlier. Sarah left behind her husband and four children. The humbling part of this story was that I got to spend a few hours each weeknight with Sarah and got to know the amazing heart she had for people and the joy she spread with her servant heart, beautiful smile, and courage, despite her difficult life. Sarah was truly loved by all who were blessed to cross her path. The children's hospital staff even held a memorial for her; her many years of service there had an impact on them. I would go to the hospital from work, tired from the day, and five minutes after being around her made me forget all about my woes and made me look at life with positivity and a smile. She had that impact on people. It was a huge lesson in attitude from the greatest teacher ever!

The next phase of life brought our family to Alberta, two provinces away, where we reside today. Stacey was hired by my brother and his new drilling company, and I pursued my career in hydraulics. Still engulfed in my bad habits of overworking and alcohol, my home life began to suffer. In 2003, Stacey and I started our own hydraulic business, building a good reputation in that industry. In the same year, our third son, Noah, was born. The destructive patterns continued, and as a result of our caustic home situation, a member of my family was negatively impacted, and I was nearly too late to respond. But my faith came through for my family, and the situation eventually was mended. The acreage life was great for a while, but the endless maintenance while still running a business had finally taken its toll. We suffered through the 2008–2010 recession, made it through, and before rehiring manpower again, decided to sell our assets, clear our debt, and work for the man again. I feel that if I had decided to continue without Stacey, we would not be together today. That was probably the best decision I ever made! I'm a slow learner, but I'm still learning.

In 2010, around the same time, my sister Rosalie passed away at the age of fifty-three due to esophageal cancer. She left a husband and seven children behind—another tough blow, especially for her family. She, also like Sarah, was an impactful leader in the community and was loved by everyone.

With the pressure of running a business removed for the next few years, things progressed as normal as we could hope. I was genuinely making an effort to be there for my family more and taking up some small hobbies such as minor gunsmithing (I even took an online course and got the certificate). The routine thing on a Saturday was to enjoy a few drinks and play in the garage with my lathe and guns. It was fun and relaxing, but I knew deep down there had to be something more. There were parts of me that still missed the hustle and bustle of my own business.

A couple of other challenging moments in my life that I would need another chapter just to elaborate on are the instant passing of my father in 2004 (he died of a severe heart attack) and the death of my mother in 2016, after five years of suffering from a stroke. Through those most brutal years of her life, I believe she positively impacted people's lives through her fight and determination.

In 2016, my life journey took a path for the better. Educating myself from books and personal mentors had me learning lessons long overdue. A few of these are the importance of family, empathy for others, and letting go of the status quo. Finally, getting my drinking under control, learning how to let status and ego not control my life, and not worrying about what people think of me are a few more things I have been working on. The list of what I learn every day keeps building up, which leads me to share my story.

## BIOGRAPHY

Adrien Fouillard has had experience in various fields of business. Some of the positions he held are a sailor in the Canadian Navy, small business owner, service manager, successful entrepreneur, and network marketer. He has sailed around the world, moved his family from coast to coast, and experienced life to the fullest along his journey. His educational achievements and accreditations include Naval Weapons Technician, Certified Fluid Power Hydraulic Specialist, Certified Engineering Technician, and Gunsmith. Adrien's proudest accomplishments are husband and father. Through many life lessons and mentorship, Adrien has been able to put things behind him that were holding him back from achieving a great life. He now believes that sharing some of those lessons could be instrumental in creating significance for others. Adrien has been married to Stacey since 1993, and they have three boys: Christian, Nathaniel, and Noah.

Connect with Adrien Fouillard via https://linktr.ee/Sailor67

CHAPTER 2

# Journey To Success

*By Matt Morris*

As a speaker and coach for the past twenty years, I've been blessed to help several thousand people become full-time entrepreneurs with hundreds in the six-figure range and over fifty documented million-dollar earners.

It's also rewarded me with a lifestyle that I never would have imagined as a boy. If you would have told me I'd be a millionaire at twenty-nine, earn eight figures in my thirties and generate several billion in sales, all while adventuring to over eighty countries by my early forties; I wouldn't have believed you.

I also never imagined I'd be blessed with a career that fills me up with such immense levels of fulfillment and significance, knowing that I've been able to assist so many others in achieving what most would consider "boundless" levels of success.

The question I'm asked all the time is . . . How?

In asking that question, most people are looking for tactics and strategies. And I'll admit, early in my coaching days, I focused my mentorship almost solely on teaching the how-tos.

Unfortunately, that made me a pretty lousy coach.

I'd give them the tactics that allowed me to become a superstar salesperson, run a multi-million dollar company, or speak powerfully from stage.

My students would apply the how-tos and come back frustrated with mediocre improvements at best.

What I failed to realize in my early coaching days is a quote from the late Brian Klemmer that says, "If how-tos were enough, we'd all be rich, skinny, and happy."

As we explore the secrets to experiencing boundless levels of success, we must first examine what keeps us bound to our current situation.

Hint: It's NOT a lack of tactics and strategies.

With a quick google search, you can find hundreds of YouTube videos and blog posts that will teach you the strategies to having six-pack abs. The reason most don't have that six-pack isn't that they don't know the how-tos.

When it comes to making your goals a reality, whether that be to have a sexy body, to become a top sales leader in your company, to start your own business, or any other worthwhile dream, the ONLY thing holding you back from achieving that goal is your mental programming.

The challenge most face in achieving a grand visionary future for themselves is the fact that it runs so completely contrary to their current vision, or identity, that's running them now.

Your current identity is made up of the beliefs you currently hold to be true about yourself. It's essentially how you genuinely see yourself.

Your personal identity subconsciously influences every decision and action you make (or don't make), thus influencing the level of success you're able to achieve.

If your personal identity is that of someone who is out of shape or overweight, you may go on streaks where you eat right and exercise vigorously, but you tend to always shift right back into your old ways. Irresistible cravings, lethargy, sleeping in, etc., are somehow always overpowering your desire to be fit.

Why is that the case?

You'll want to write this down.

**The Law of Commitment and Consistency**

*The law of commitment and consistency says that we will remain committed to remaining consistent with who we genuinely believe we are.*

That being true, we must understand that in order to change our results, we have to change the beliefs we have about ourselves.

Let's take a deep dive into beliefs.

Take a look at the middle three letters of the word "beliefs," and what word do you see?

LIE

Consider for a moment that the story (the beliefs) you've been telling yourself about who you are as a person are simply lies you've made up.

Stories you may have accepted as "fact" like you're:

- Shy
- Self-conscious
- Lacking self-confidence
- Not a morning person
- Afraid of public speaking
- Not a good communicator
- Not as smart as the others

Would it be empowering to know that any of the negative beliefs above, along with countless others, are nothing more than lies you created subconsciously through a belief-building process you went through and didn't even know you were going through it?

What makes me so certain these "character traits" are lies? Because I had all of those beliefs about myself that I once accepted as fact.

Today, if you told me I was any of those things, I would laugh in your face because it would be completely absurd in my mind to accept any of those as true.

If you're willing to take a journey with me, I'll show you how I literally rewrote my entire identity from a broke, scarcity-filled, self-conscious young man into a confident and powerful multi-millionaire.

I'm here to tell you that whatever limiting beliefs you've created for yourself are absolute and total crap. I'm proof of it and many of those I've mentored for the past twenty years are proof of it.

I don't know what lies about yourself you've accepted as fact, but I know beyond a shadow of a doubt that, at your core, you are not a bad communicator, you are not unworthy of finding love, you are not a failure, you are not destined to always struggle, or any other negative belief.

Whatever they might be, you have the power to change those disempowering beliefs that serve only to limit the amount of success and personal fulfillment you experience.

If your current beliefs are what determine your success, the big question becomes how do you change your beliefs to create the results you want?

Before we answer that question, you first need to understand what shapes your beliefs in the first place. What has caused you to hold the beliefs that you do? Understanding where they came from will help you change them.

The belief building process you went through to come up with the beliefs you currently hold to be true have been shaped by three main factors:

1. Experiences
2. External programming
3. Internal programming

**Experiences:**

Every experience you've ever been through has been forever deposited and stored somewhere in your subconscious mind.

Maybe you were teased as a kid in school because you stuttered, and now you believe you're a poor communicator. Maybe you were laughed at in class as a kid for giving the wrong answer, and you took on a belief that you're not as smart as the other kids. Maybe you made a few horrible business choices when you were first starting out, and now you think you're lousy in business.

Whether you've realized it before now or not, those deposits were the first major factor that gave you the foundation of your identity.

Here's the way it works . . .

An event happens and then you make up a story (a belief) about what that event means.

Most of us tend to create a negative meaning based on what we perceive to be a negative experience. We create a victim story—I'm not loved because my parents abused me or left me. I'm a terrible business person because I failed for five years. People are not trustworthy because my business partner stole from me (all personal stories I made up at one point).

Think about some examples from your past. Can you think of some examples of events where you created a negative belief?

***Real power comes from understanding that nothing has meaning until we give it meaning.***

Events are neutral. It's the story we make up from the event that holds all the power. Rather than the victim story you may have been running in your mind, how can you create a new and empowering meaning based on that experience?

Understand—you have the power to choose. Victim or Victor. Which will it be?

**External Programming:**

Whether you want to believe this or not, you've been programmed.

Your parents programmed you as a child to believe certain things about yourself, other people, money, religion, and many other things.

The school system, your friends, the media, television, and other factors have programmed you to believe many of the things you do today.

Some of this programming has likely been healthy and gotten you to where you are and built you into the person you are today. Unfortunately, we also all have some less than empowering beliefs, and associated fears, that we've adopted as well from that external programming.

By the time you were two years old, you heard the word no thousands of times more than you heard the word yes. It's no wonder so many people, when presented with an opportunity to start a business or take on a challenge, are paralyzed with fear and are hesitant to take action.

At some point in your life, you've most likely faced a moment where someone said something negative to you or doubted your ability, without even meaning to. For a lot of people, that first comes from their parents and family members.

The things that people say to you, whether they intentionally mean harm or not, can profoundly shape who you are—*but only if you let it.* You obviously can't go back into the past and change the negative things you've heard, but you can make the decision right now to no longer let those things define you.

You can recognize that what someone says about you has no basis in reality unless you *choose* to believe it. It's a choice. A choice you can start making right now, today, to say **no more**.

**Internal Programming:**

More than your experiences and more than the voices of the people around you, the greatest and most powerful way your beliefs are shaped is from your internal programming. Thankfully, it's also the mechanism you have the most control over.

Every word that comes out of your mouth and every thought that comes out of your mind serves as a programming tool. Those thoughts and words get entered into your subconscious mind and then work to create your habitual routines and mental thought patterns.

Psychologists who study brain science agree that your subconscious mind is infinitely more powerful than your conscious mind. The subconscious is the driving force behind your belief system and your identity.

The subconscious mind has a goal that can serve you negatively or positively. That goal is to keep you in line with your identity. Remember the law of commitment and consistency?

If, based on your regular programming, you tell yourself you're broke, you're tired, and you suck as an entrepreneur, your subconscious mind figures out a way to keep you consistent with that programming.

If, however, you continually tell yourself you're wealthy, you're energized, and you're an amazing entrepreneur, your subconscious mind begins doing everything in its power to create *that* reality.

Here's the best way to understand it.

**Whatever you say about yourself makes it more true.**

If you say, *"I'm an idiot,"* you become more of an idiot. If you say, *"I'm a genius,"* you become more of a genius.

Your consistent programming creates your identity.

Here's the trick; your subconscious mind does not know the difference between the truth and a lie. It simply does its best to carry out exactly what you've programmed it to believe.

So when you say, "I'm sexy, I'm confident, I'm a millionaire," your conscious mind might be telling you you're full of it, but your subconscious mind, which is where the true power lies, will take that as a command and start working out a way for you to be all of those things.

The key to reprogramming your subconscious and changing your deep-seeded beliefs is to change your deposits. You do this by constantly filling your subconscious mind with empowering, uplifting, and motivating thoughts and words.

If you continually profess what you don't want, or focus on the things you don't have or aren't, then you actually attract more of that negativity and continue to reinforce more of that personal identity. **What you focus on expands**.

## BIOGRAPHY

Author of the international bestseller, *The Unemployed Millionaire*, Matt Morris began his career as a serial entrepreneur aged eighteen. Since then, he has generated over $1.5 billion through his sales organizations, with a total of over one million customers worldwide. As a self-made millionaire and one of the top internet and network marketing experts, he's been featured on international radio and television and spoken from platforms to audiences in over twenty-five countries around the world. And now, as the founder of Success Publishing, he co-authors with leading experts from every walk of life.

Contact Matt Morris via http://www.MattMorris.com

CHAPTER 3

# Scared Shitless

*By Steve Moreland*

How do you keep from tossing in the towel at age thirty-five because a twenty-five-year prison sentence for crimes you did not commit is just a bridge too far?

As I read G. K. Chesterton's book *Orthodoxy* one night inside that icy, cement cell, it felt like a ray of hope had pierced the dark maze that often felt like a grave.

> "Courage is almost a contradiction in terms. Valor means a strong desire to live, taking the form of a readiness to die. 'He that will lose his life, the same shall save it' is not a piece of mysticism for saints and heroes. It is a piece of everyday advice for sailors and mountaineers. It might be printed in an Alpine guide or a drill book. The paradox is the whole principle of courage, even of quite earthly or quite brutal courage. A man cut off by the sea may save his life if he will risk it on the precipice. He can only get away from death by continually stepping within an inch of it. A soldier surrounded by enemies, if he is to cut his way out, needs to combine a strong desire for living with a strange carelessness about dying. He must not merely cling to life, for then he will be a coward, and will not

> escape. He must not merely wait for death, for then he will be a suicide, and will not escape. ***He must seek his life in a spirit of furious indifference to it; he must desire life like water and yet drink death like wine.***"

I was trained to believe the test of a man is what it takes to stop him. Grit is what it's called in Texas. It's brutal. And it's not about anything other than performance, because no one cares to hear your weak, sniveling excuses. So, you grow up learning how to numb the pain of the sun burning the back of your neck and from suffocating in the 110-degree, breezeless terrain. You get used to the burnt grass, the scrub pines, the desolate landscapes, and the intolerant demands for excellence from a decorated war hero called Dad.

The first time I came home beat up at age twelve by three fourteen-year-olds, I expected some sympathy. But boy, was I mistaken! I revered his service to our country as a Marine, whose last mission to destroy an embedded bunker on the DMZ in Vietnam in 1968 resulted in half the recon team KIA (killed in action) and the other half WIA (wounded in action). Valor, in the face of overwhelming force, had caused his thousand-yard stare that freaked out most people. But to me, he was Dad.

After explaining how I'd been jumped by three bigger boys, he began demonstrating techniques to snap their necks or break their spines. In utter disbelief, I argued that I could not murder them. And then his emotionless response caused my heart to sink, when he replied, "Okay, then, if you come home beaten up again, I'll beat you worse."

Talk about jumping from the frying pan and into the fire! My heart stopped. I had gone to him for help. But instead, I was sure my days on earth were numbered because I cried to the wrong Marine. And yet, the next time Jeff Hayes came after me, I reacted with a level of force that terrified me. It wasn't pretty. It wasn't Bruce Lee level awesome. It came out of sheer terror. What some call scared shitless! And to my amazement, it worked.

In life, you're first given the test, later the lesson.

Life has rarely made sense to me. You'd think we'd get an instruction manual explaining how to solve life's challenges. Instead, we often get advice from "armchair quarterbacks" who hide from any real risk because they've never learned how to perform the common (duties) under uncommon conditions. They give you tons of "ideas" that are as worthless as those theories blathered by our business professors, who have never spent a single day performing in the real world.

He'd sadly pronounced at an early age that I didn't have a lick of athletic talent, so I was ordered to make first-squad by out-practicing everyone else. I worked extra hard until the coach felt guilty for not letting me play—raw discipline fueled by being scared shitless not to measure up to Dad's expectations.

Years later, I found myself fighting in martial art tournaments for the thrill and outrunning state troopers on my Kawasaki Ninja motorcycle at over 100 MPH to supply that "fix" of scared shitlessness. Later, it was fighting in parking lots against half of the offensive line of some goat-roping town out in the sticks nearby or joy-riding in stolen cars. Recklessness had become my drug of choice.

Then, as fate would have it, I accidentally won academic scholarships and Dad forbade me to enlist in his beloved Marine Corps. His "change of orders" was to get a degree from those professors with little to no experience, and return to the Corps and lead as an officer instead of battle-proven Gunnery Sergeant. So, what did I do but blow up my scholarships with my disrespectful comments to the dean of business when he refused my challenge to compare his tax return to mine. You see, in 1986, I'd reported over $40,000 from my part-time grass mowing business when I wasn't working out, playing point guard on the squad, or traveling with the Taekwondo team. So, after my BCD (Marine lingo for a "bad conduct discharge") from my scholarships, I sought out a new challenge to redeem myself in the eyes of the Marine I feared I could never equal in acts of valor.

I ran headfirst into corporate America after watching the movie *Wall Street*. Though I outperformed the guys with the degrees (that I secretly envied), my addiction demanded more. So I became a workaholic. And when the pedigreed boys laughed me out of their Monday morning sales meetings for my atypical marketing ideas, I didn't curl up in a fetal position like most folks would. I got angry, crazy-mad with revenge. I showed up earlier, stayed later, and worked all weekend. I then added to my regimen the discipline of listening to personal mindset development cassette tapes. One after another, while speeding all over Dallas until that wasn't enough. So I went to sleep with more subliminal tapes playing in the background—scared shitless that my lack of natural talent would prove me unworthy by comparison. I was determined to train my mind to think better, react faster, and perform with less apprehension of risks. To win, or die trying . . . if that's what it took!

And it worked! I'd traded in my dream of becoming a lifer as a gunnery sergeant in the U.S. Marine Corps, like Clint Eastwood's character in *Heartbreak Ridge,* to become Bud Fox in the 1985 film *Wall Street*. I ranked as the top producer in several Fortune 500 companies before I was twenty-five, started my own brokerage agency for a Canadian insurance juggernaut shortly thereafter, and fearlessly catapulted myself into the shark-infested waters of offshore private banking and venture capital investing, all before age thirty. I was prouder of my titles than my eight-figure net worth: director of offshore operations for my mentor's hedge fund based in Turks and Caicos, president of a fifty-eight-office trust and accounting firm based in Utah, and co-principal in a pre-IPO SaaS technology company in California.

And then the phone call came the day after returning home from our international shareholder's event in Vegas. The voice rambled on about the Feds raiding our offices, freezing all our accounts, and the founder being held in his house at gunpoint.

Since I was under the assumption that we'd been attacked without any justification and because I was being groomed to take over the reins of the company in the next ten years, technically, I was now in command. So, everyone was waiting for my decisions amidst the absolute chaos.

Finally, war had found me. I was going to get my chance to prove my worth. And I performed with ice in my veins.

I defended our operation to prevent further wrongdoing by what I believed to be just another Jeff Hays bully coming to kick my ass. Within twenty-four hours, I had secured our offshore holdings that hadn't been discovered, relocated our command and control to a foreign country, and caused several thousand investors to literally disappear from the open internet and onto an encrypted server based in Ireland. In Dad's lingo, I'd successfully hardened communications, reinforced HQ, and secured our resources.

And boy, did I piss off the wrong gang of bullies!

By July 2002, I was inside a ten-week federal money-laundering and investment fraud trial. The prior fourteen months from federal detention in Seattle was a blur of filing motions against the U.S. attorneys, though I'd never been to law school. And by September, I was taking the stand to fight the senior prosecutor, *mano a mano*. Many of the other co-defendants had lied because they were scared shitless and had taken plea bargains to reduce their prison sentences to under five years. I refused, purely out of principle, even ignoring a direct order from Dad to break our family honor code and take the ten-year plea bargain deal.

> "A man is never more than a man than when he embraces an adventure beyond his control, or when he walks into a battle he isn't sure of winning."—John Eldridge

In the middle of such extreme risk, there's no such thing as fearlessness: There's feeling the fear and acting the right way regardless. So I learned that real performance is just continuing to engage, even when you're scared shitless. It's finding that space called faith. Not faith in the Creator but faith in your ability to endure levels of agony that would cause the hearts of most to seize up.

In Will Smith's movie *After Earth*, he plays the character of a valiant general attempting to guide his son on a perilous mission. His son had already failed Ranger school, but now their lives depended on him doing the impossible.

> "Fear is not real. The only place that fear can exist is in our thoughts of the future. It is a product of our imagination, causing us to fear things that do not at present, and may not, ever exist. That is near insanity. Do not misunderstand me, danger is very real. But fear is a choice."

I lost at trial! Yet I continued my mission, fighting another year from detention, only to secure a seemingly minor win of a 292-month sentence instead of the life sentence in federal prison that the gang of bullies requested from the judge. When I walked onto my first yard in Beaumont, Texas, in October 2003, I was nicknamed "the yacht man" because of my once-upon-a-time wealth. It would eventually become "Sergeant Slaughter."

Amid the daily struggle against life's scum and with zero reinforcements, I secured three consecutive wins in the circuit appellate courts, more than any other white-collar, first-time, non-violent offender in history. But the real trophy was reversing my own case in the United States Supreme Court in 2009. And while fighting these near-impossible obstacles, the mother of my children turned on me during an ugly divorce and attempted to take away my rights as a father and erase me from the lives of my two children. Her father warned her, "Dumb mistake, Steve doesn't surrender!"

For 5,544 days, I marched across hell. The demons walking the halls at night relentlessly whispered that I was a fool, insane, exhibiting conduct unbecoming of a father and husband. And maybe they were right. Perhaps I should have acted like a coward and broken our family's honor code by lying about doing something I did not. Perhaps I should have set the example for my children by giving lip service to my creed but breaking weak when life got ugly. That's what most others would have done . . . and then justified their cowardice with lame excuses.

From experience, not theory, I can tell you there are no perfect solutions to impossible scenarios. So I'll share with you how I reasoned why I was being tortured. I penned an essay in 2007 entitled *A Perfect Imperfection* and published it on my blog from prison. My blog is called Tsyo Matte, samurai lingo for "Be Strong!" (https://tsuyomatte.wordpress.com/).

> Therefore we must ask ourselves what makes our heroes heroic? Are they perfect? Hardly. What makes a hero so heroic isn't that he's perfect, but that he is imperfect. A hero is a person who overcomes his own limitations, transcends his weaknesses, and stands his ground when most retreat to excuses. He becomes, in effect, a perfect imperfection, just as a perfect storm achieves its terrifying strength through a perfect combination of imperfect—that is to say, disorderly—elements. Valor can only be found in these most imperfect of places, confusing places, that leave behind clues of "how" the few performed, and more importantly, "why." These characteristics conceal themselves; they hide within enigmas and paradoxes—buried inside legends, lore, and myths. And the cardinal paradox cloaking itself within the imperfect chaos of battle is a pure and relentless allegiance to a sacred cause, a meaning so perfect, the warrior "performs the ordinary under extraordinary conditions."

In that lonely trek across my desert challenge, life became really simple. I came to understand that the test of one's caliber is what it takes to stop you. In those endless days and darkest nights, I found a few lines from the book *Endurance: Shackleton's Incredible Voyage* that transformed the hopelessness into meaningfulness. After seventeen months stranded on the Antarctic ice shelf, twenty-eight survivors made it back to civilization. While reading their journal entries, I noticed that, in some ways, they had come to know themselves better in that lonely world of ice and emptiness. They had achieved at least a limited kind of contentment. One unique entry spoke volumes. "***We'd been tested . . . and found not wanting.***" It went on to describe how they felt that special kind of pride of a person who, in a foolish moment, accepts an impossible dare—then pulls it off to perfection.

This secret that I've shared with you can carry you through life's impossible missions. It begins with a commitment to principle, to a code, that dishonoring scares you shitless. The agony that you'll suffer during your commitment must torture your soul less than standing in front of the ultimate tribunal to account for your conduct under duress.

But beyond that commitment to purpose and principle, you must possess something called passion. In my case, that passion was the fatherly love for my children. In my mind, again and again, two films replayed. One, my children standing over my headstone that they'd chosen, "Here lies an average man, like everyone else." And the other, just one word. "Worthy."

Passion fueled this father's trek across hell. It was about being scared shitless to account to my children that I'd cowered to the bully called fate and dishonored them by my fear. This fueled me to rise just one more time and trust the Creator that only through being scared shitless can we be *tested . . . and found not wanting.*

## BIOGRAPHY

As a human that has intimately danced with tragedy, injustice, and anguish, Steve lives to inspire the few destined to impact the many. He's director of performance for Success Publishing where he coaches authors inside his best friend's Mastermind group to "embrace the suck" by expressing courageous vulnerability in telling their Stories.

Mission: To deliberately cause affirmative outcomes that would not have occurred otherwise
Slogan: *Chance favors the prepared*
Mantra: No one left behind

Connect with Steve via LinkTree: https://linktr.ee/steve_moreland

CHAPTER 4

# My American Dream

*By Alden Porter III*

Does it bother you that most people in our country—the richest country on the planet—cannot afford to pay cash for a new car tire? Are you one of those people? According to Bankrate.com, only thirty-seven percent of Americans have enough savings to cover a $500 emergency.[1]

It sure bugs me! It took me a very long time to learn how money works. I had to learn the hard way.

I grew up in a union household in the Detroit area during the 1960s and 1970s. I lived a typical suburban life until my parents got divorced when I was sixteen. Financially, it was devastating, as my two younger sisters and I moved with my mom. We survived just fine, but our standard of living did drop quite a bit.

As I reflect on the role of money in my life, I remember the first significant money event I experienced. I was either ten or eleven years old, and I had a paper route. Today, if people even choose to receive a physical newspaper, it is likely delivered by an adult in a car or truck. In my day, kids used their bicycles to deliver to many houses in one or more neighborhoods around their home. Almost everyone got a newspaper seven days a week.

---

[1] Sheyna Steiner, "Survey: How Do You Pay For Unexpected Expenses?" Bankrate, January 6, 2016, https://www.bankrate.com/banking/savings/survey-how-americans-contend-with-unexpected-expenses/.

One of my responsibilities was to collect the weekly subscription fee from my customers. Most people paid in cash. One time, I took all the cash and spent a few hours at the local arcade playing pinball. My parents were furious! Of course, they had to repay the newspaper company. This was the first time I realized money could have a major impact on a person's life.

I joined the U.S. Navy right after high school. Even though I was an Eagle Scout by then and had earned my personal finance merit badge, I still could not handle money. I was a regular with the "slush fund" sailors on board. Boy, did they see me coming from a mile away! Here's how it worked. I would borrow money that I needed to pay back next paycheck. I got into a never-ending cycle where I would be paying my entire paycheck out for loans each payday and then need to borrow again. The going rate was to borrow $20 and pay back $30! Wow! In retrospect, I cannot believe I did that. But my Navy days were all about work and partying, giving no thought to the future whatsoever.

Another significant money incident comes to mind. I remember my wife and I walking down the beach with friends in Southern California after taking our five-year-old to Disneyland. During that walk on the beach, I remember saying that "I don't care about taking money from my credit card. I'll not even live long enough to pay it back!" Oh boy, I cannot believe I felt that way. It took around ten years to pay off that decision to impulsively take several hundred dollars in a credit card cash advance.

Moving on a few years, my wife and I moved from California to Michigan with our three kids. I was still not managing my money well. I had to work a full-time day job and get up at 3 am every morning, seven days a week, to deliver the *New York Times* for $180 in cash every week.

I eventually landed a great corporate job where I got a raise every year and a bonus most years. Things got better as we managed to buy our first house. We were so happy! Of course, we remodeled the house on credit cards. It took me a long time to learn to do better. We went through a credit counseling program and eliminated our debt! We were then able to move into a newly built house on the other side of our town. I got credit cards again with the reasoning that I had to finish and furnish my brand-new home. Even after the first go around with credit card debt, I used the new credit cards poorly.

Slow learner, that's me! Well, not really. I have three college degrees and have always done rather well academically. I feel like I was totally into the "keeping-up-with-Jones's" or even "surpassing-the-Jones's" mentality. I fell into the trap of wanting many material things: a nice big house, fancy new cars, and big vacations. Although there is nothing wrong with any of these things, I did wrong to finance them on credit cards. I was living my American Dream but with financial insecurity and stress lurking in the background.

Then it all came crashing down: my wife lost her job. That was enough to push us over the edge. You may have experienced asking a credit card company for help. They are not very interested. They just want you to pay. You cannot blame them. You agreed to pay them under the terms and conditions of their credit card. We were in a financial tailspin. It was quite the wake-up call for me. It was and still is very embarrassing. I had a great job and made very good money. But I did not know how money worked. I hard to learn the hard way.

Then, another event that served as a strong financial wake-up call took place. My father's third wife passed away, and he decided to come live with us. As his mental health declined, I took over his financial affairs. I was stunned to learn that he had no retirement savings—only a very small pension and government benefits. I knew he had inherited a substantial sum from his parents, but he did not know how money worked. I guess it is true that "the acorn does not fall far from the tree."

Having always been a good student, I started an intensive study about money.

My wife and I attended a very well-known money expert's education program. I learned there that before World War II, credit like we know it today—installment credit—did not exist. People would save money until they had enough to buy whatever they wanted. The invention of installment credit was a great boon to the economy as people could now pay over time and not have to wait for what they desired. Combine that "easy money" with incessant advertising, and just about everyone jumped on the installment credit bandwagon.

This new credit system worked very well in the beginning. But eventually, it turned into what we have today: a massive national credit card and installment debt of several billion dollars annually. As my knowledge increased, I became convinced that using cash and saving for things I wanted was a better way to handle my money than I had ever done.

I was fortunate enough to join a major corporation before they stopped offering a pension plan and moved solely to a 401K retirement approach for their employees. When it came time to choose my pension options, I did what pretty much everyone did: I chose a survivor option for my wife, which lowered my pension payment. I did not choose the lump sum option, opting for the lifetime monthly payments instead. As I embarked on my journey to improve my knowledge about how money works, I learned that I did nothing wrong with my pension choice. But, oh my, I could have done so much better. This is just one of the reasons I am now on the mission to educate as many people as possible about how money works. I desire to teach everyone this information known by rich people forever. It is one of the ways the rich stay rich!

How do you feel about money in your life? Is it a source of stress? Do you live paycheck-to-paycheck? Do you save enough money? Are you prepared or preparing for retirement? Do you feel guilty for not knowing how to manage your money better?

These are all questions I asked myself. These questions are where I began my research on the topic of money. Wow, talk about drinking from a firehose! I was initially very overwhelmed. One of the most valuable things I learned in college was how to figure relevant or germane information on what I wanted to learn from numerous sources. That skill has served me well on this educational journey.

There sure is plenty of information about money available these days. There are many conflicting views. For example, there are approaches that favor investing in stocks or bonds, government tax-deferred plans like

IRAs and 401Ks, a wide variety of insurances for just about everything, and many other ideas about what a person should do with their money. It can be, let's face it, confusing! How do you get a handle on this topic?

Honestly, most of the advice out there has worked for someone at some time. If you want to determine what is best for you, this is where persistence pays off. The key is: DO NOT QUIT. This advice can be useful in every area of life. DO NOT BE DISCOURAGED. I know it's easier said than done. So, what has been my secret? Well, there is no secret. I was raised to believe that I could do anything. Thanks, Mom! I think this has been instrumental in my success in life.

I have had plenty of other failures in life—so many that I could write an entire book on the topic. It has been said better by others, but it is true: you must learn from your mistakes. I know it is now a cliché to say such a thing. It is still true, though.

Anybody can learn about how money works. It is much easier than you think. The concepts are not difficult to understand. They have just never been taught to average families. My mission is to provide basic financial education to as many people as I can for as long as possible. I'm in what one could call the "second half of life." I do not need to earn more money. That does not mean that I don't want to earn. In fact, I continue to earn money in my "retirement." The key is to enjoy what I am doing. I am a teacher for teachers. I cannot think of a more important topic that EVERYONE needs to know more about, regardless of age, income, or stage of life.

It has been said, "If you chase money, it will run from you." Believe it.

# BIOGRAPHY

Alden Porter is a Financial Professional and Small Business Coach. He took an early retirement from a major corporation a few years ago and decided to get into the business of helping others. Alden has three college degrees, over two decades of corporate experience, and over a decade of experience as a small business owner. After completing a long journey to financial success and security in his life, Alden is determined to help others learn "how money works." He is motivated by teaching others how to achieve what he has done, doing it better and more quickly. He has completed intensive study and licensing in financial services. He now works with others to share his knowledge, experience, expertise, and wisdom with those who wish to live their life more abundantly.

Connect with Alden Porter via https://linktr.ee/Alden3

CHAPTER 5

# What Full Commitment Can Truly Do

*By Caroline Lekanyang*

When all is said and done, a lot more gets said than done. I had an obligation to do something about my life: it had to change for the better!

Have you ever wondered why some people become immensely successful while others work just as hard but achieve little to nothing? Why is that? Consistency. That is the key to success, no matter what you are doing.

For fifteen years, I worked as a teacher. For over half of those years, I was living a fake life. Most of the time, I would do things to please others and not myself.

Do you know it is easy to live a lifestyle beyond what one can truly afford? Buying on credit has become a norm. But just because it seems normal, it doesn't mean we should do it. I found myself buried in this kind of life.

There were warning signs I was living beyond my means. This was because I let fear dictate my spending. I neither set a budget nor kept money aside for any emergencies.

For several years, I was trading true happiness for momentary pleasures. I would often find myself engaging in self-defeating habits that would thwart my success and ability to reach my goals.

They say, 'Fake it till you make it,' but my lifestyle took it up a notch. Was I like the many people who cared too much about what other people thought and not enough about my values? Well, I guess I was!

Have you, at some point, found yourself spending money on things to help you cope with your life? This might include, but not be limited to, buying expensive foods, new clothes, cars on credit, and even taking vacations on credit!

I found myself living a life of debt. I found myself owing money to my friends, family, and banks. I started to try this and that, buy and sell clothes and, at some point, vegetables, to make the extra income to supplement my salary. I was drowning in debt for more than five years, and nothing I tried seemed to help.

How was I going to get up because I could stay there forever? This is the question I kept asking myself for more than five years as I drowned myself in heavy debt. But one day, I decided to step up. I decided to live more authentically and made a choice to accept myself, including my flaws and strengths. I learnt that to achieve my dream of tomorrow, I need to take the necessary steps today. So, I acted!

Many opportunities presented themselves to me, and I needed to act. I decided to quit my teaching job and went into network marketing. Many of my friends kept asking me, 'How long will it take for you to become successful with what you are doing and change your life?' I didn't have the best answer, but I kept telling them, 'I don't know. It depends.'

For the past four years, I have been in network marketing, and some of the people who want to do what I am doing would frequently ask me: 'When can I expect to start earning a lot of money in network marketing?' The answer I always give them is the same: 'It depends.' 'Depends on what?' would be the follow-up question. It depends on how much time you are willing to put into learning *consistently*.

Consistency is a crucial ingredient for success; it leads to habits. Habits shape our everyday actions. Action leads to success. As Anthony Robbins said: "It's not what we do once in a while that shapes our lives. It's what we do consistently."[2]

---

2   "A Quote by Anthony Robbins," Goodreads (Goodreads), accessed June 3, 2021, https://www.goodreads.com/quotes/328976-it-s-not-what-we-do-once-in-a-while-that.

Have you ever wondered how people in sports achieve their goals? They ensure that their training is consistent. Consistency in training separates the good from the great. Consistency is a crucial part of training. The same principle applies to other areas where success is the desired outcome.

It is important for me, even now, to continue doing what I am doing repeatedly. Repetition and consistency are key in achieving gains. One must understand that results aren't achieved overnight but rather after months, or maybe even years, of sticking to the same routine.

It is challenging to execute consistency because of its repetitive nature; it can be a bit monotonous, and it takes time and patience to see results. But one must understand the process and the purpose behind what they are doing.

John Maxwell said, "Small disciplines repeated with consistency every day lead to great achievement gained slowly over time."[3] For almost four years, I learnt how to change my behaviour and get comfortable with it. Doing the little things repeatedly helped me to accomplish the goals that I have always wanted to achieve.

Are you that person who maybe wants to lose weight or start your own business? Maybe you'd like to learn swimming or something exciting, but then the excitement just dies off? Lack of consistency might be the one thing that is keeping you from achieving your goals.

Consistency can do tremendous things in one's life. It can allow a person to know if something works or not. You cannot say you can't swim when you've practiced only once or twice. It takes time and practice to develop a skill.

You can plan the best business plans, but without consistency, it is set up for failure. For me to be consistent in what I do, I had to cultivate the right mindset. They say good habits start in the mind.

---

3 "A Quote from The 15 Invaluable Laws of Growth," Goodreads (Goodreads), accessed June 3, 2021, https://www.goodreads.com/quotes/748932-small-disciplines-repeated-with-consistency-every-day-lead-to-great.

But why is it so hard to build a routine—not just any routine, but a consistent one? Is it because there are numerous distractions along the way? Or maybe people are just too busy? Or maybe they are procrastinating? Is it because a routine is simply boring? Well, there are many reasons, but the fact of the matter is that building a habit is hard, and most people want to take the easy road. Perhaps it's wired in our human nature to take the easy route, which saves both energy and time. This route, however, doesn't lead to *lasting* success.

After years of working and not achieving financial independence, I realized I should take action and be consistent with my goals. I learnt that to achieve anything of value and meaning meant that I needed to be consistent long term.

Do people who want to get into great shape workout only once a week or once a month and expect to get an amazing body? No, it doesn't work that way. They have to be consistent every single day. Every day, they must attempt to progress towards their goals: working out, following a healthy eating program, and being consistent with that for over several months or years will lead to achieving their goals.

The same can be applied to building a business and making money. You have to work on the money-making activity with consistency every day.

Whatever your routine is, you need to be consistent, and those little actions you take will eventually lead to big results later down the road.

Consistency is paramount. At some point, I would get distracted by what is happening around me and fall off track. But you know what? I never beat myself up for it. I understood that the bigger someone plays, the bigger their breakdown. I never thought of quitting. In fact, I took quitting off the table! The most important thing was to get myself up and back on track. I jumped on the wagon again and focused on being consistent after that.

I have a big 'why,' and I keep my eyes on it every day. I have a clear, compelling reason why I have to do what I am doing. I need financial independence. This is why I take consistency as something very important that can help me achieve my goal.

As humans, we are limited when it comes to willpower and discipline. It is important to note that we cannot focus our energy on two or more things, or habits, at the same time. Otherwise, we will fail at both. Therefore, I pick one battle at a time. I focus on one thing and work on that. Once I am now good at it, I pick the other thing and work on it.

Steven Covey says, "The key is not to prioritize what's on your schedule, but to schedule your priorities."[4] I decided to quit my teaching job to focus on what can bring me true financial independence because I wanted to have something consistent in my life; I wanted to build my whole life around it and not try to fit it in my life. So, for me, to be consistent, I had to schedule my priorities and do whatever it took to protect my dreams.

We all have dreams and visions of our version of an ideal life. Most of us never make it happen because we don't protect our dreams so that they flourish and grow. We give up all too soon and easily. We should learn to take little actions daily to germinate our dreams, grow them a bit, and let them take root. This can only happen when we are specific and consistent.

Another important thing I have learnt to do is to ignore my feelings. Yes, I have often ignored the small voice in my head that says, 'I do not feel like doing it.' Is it not true that every time you want to work on something worthwhile—working out, meditation, reading a book, or other productive activities—that you hear a voice that says, 'I don't feel like it!' I have trained myself to override that voice because I know the power of consistency.

Remember that success does not come from what you do occasionally; it comes from what you do consistently.

You can work any business, full-time or part-time. If you decide to do it part-time, it should be *part-time* and not *sometimes*. You must be deliberate and purposeful with the hours you put into your business. You must be ready to focus on money-generating activities.

---

4   "Stephen Covey Quotes," BrainyQuote (Xplore), accessed June 3, 2021, https://www.brainyquote.com/quotes/stephen_covey_133504.

I started working my part-time business and consistently worked three to five hours every day after work. Nine months into my business, I was able to walk away from my full-time teaching job. I became in charge of my time and made more money by working from home at my own pace.

I know many people think they are too overwhelmed and can't fit anything more into their lives. Remember, I had three to five hours every day after work to learn and work towards my goal. It is essential to see the bigger picture. With simply an hour or two of daily work, you can make something meaningful for yourself and others. But you cannot work on it tepidly. You must be prepared to work *every* day! Consistency is key.

What separates failure from success is consistency. Consistency is the key to success. Consistency leads to habits, and habits form our daily actions. These everyday actions lead to success.

The power of consistency is profound. Doing the little things repeatedly helped me accomplish some of my dearest life goals.

Life is all about commitment. Every decision and action matters—everything matters. Success depends on what you do and how well you do it consistently. Consistency is the key to all success.

## BIOGRAPHY

Carol Lekanyang is a former secondary school teacher who began her multilevel marketing journey to earn extra income. She quickly earned more than her teaching salary. After firing her boss, she is now living life on her own terms. Carol has the passion for sharing her success system with others to help, inspire, motivate, and encourage them to achieve their goals and believe that attaining the impossible is truly possible. Her visionary leadership has helped many around her to achieve massive success in business.

Connect with Carol Lekanyang via https://linktr.ee/carolmillionaire

CHAPTER 6

# Bullied, But Never Beaten!

*By Cayle Lawrence*

I'm about to share with you the experiences that got me through my early years and how being bullied made me the strong, thick-skinned woman I am today. My dad's favourite joke to this day is that he believes I was switched at birth and that he and mum were sent home with the wrong baby because there was no way in hell this strong-willed, outgoing, defiant girl could have been his daughter. I was a difficult baby, toddler, child, and teenager! And I didn't "become good" until I was nineteen and moved out of the house. When my now-husband, Ben, asked my dad's permission to marry me, his famous words were: "There's a no returns policy!" And even then, I still don't think Ben fully understood what he'd gotten himself into.

Have you ever come across a name you can't spell, pronounce, or are simply too scared to attempt saying? I have. It's my name: Cayle! Yep, my first name. And, my god, did I have a rough time growing up with it. I actually still do, thirty-two years later! I'm sure Mum and Dad could have imagined every possible scenario for me with a name like Cayle, including things that kids could pick on me for. Cayle the snail and Cayle the whale were two popular ones. But what I haven't shared with you yet is my maiden name: Crawley. My birth name was Cayle Crawley. I feel my fate was sealed at a very young age; I was an easy target, as my dad would say.

My dad, Kevin, had a pretty normal first name. Growing up with a surname like Crawley, he copped it as well. Dad's strategy was to start "picking on me" like kids would when I got to school. He did this to prepare me. So, I immediately got the nickname "Creepy Crawley" from him—because that's what people used to call him.

I grew up in the little town of Kurri Kurri (which lies approximately ninety-one miles north of Sydney, Australia)—a town that was founded in 1902 with the land built to service the local coal mining communities. For me, though, this was where the bullying started—at the tender time of primary school. Kids loved to use the overused rhyming techniques on me: Cayle the whale; Cayle the snail; Cayle, get the mail; and Cayle will go to jail. When you think about it, HOW MANY THINGS RHYME WITH CAYLE?

Unfortunately, it didn't end there. In retrospect, those were the easy days.

You see, as I got older, into my early teens, the bullying became worse…a lot worse! The name-calling expanded from my first and maiden name to hurtful slander because of my appearance: short, brown hair, a birthmark on my face, and being "blessed" (I use that term loosely) with a large chest. To be honest, I absolutely hated my appearance.

They had me believing that I fell off the ugly tree and hit every branch on the way down. I was a sl#t; I was a wh##e. I was this, and I was that, all because of how I looked. It had NOTHING to do with the person I was. And as time went on, I honestly believed that there was something wrong with me. I had MAJOR insecurities about my appearance, and unfortunately, I still haven't been able to completely shake those self-sabotaging thoughts to this day. My husband always tells me I'm beautiful; I just wish I could see myself through his eyes.

I can't even recall the number of times I was intimidated by bullies giving me empty threats like they were going to bash me. I think what got me through was—you guessed it—that strong personality I possessed. I was never one to throw punches, but I most definitely wouldn't bite my tongue with anyone. It was a game to them. They'd hurt me so much that I would eventually snap, telling them what I thought and what they could do with their opinions of me. I was adding fuel to their fire. They'd get a rise out of me, and their mission would be complete. But I couldn't help myself! I'm not the kind of person who sits back and stays silent!

This behaviour would grind my dad's gears big time! He'd hate to see his daughter hurt, crying, and an emotional wreck. But as a parent, what could you do? You aren't meant to stand up to those bullies yourself. After all, they're kids!

During my high school years, I ended up having more male than female friends.

Why? Because I just couldn't handle the b*****ness. I was sick to death of being told I was fat and ugly.

I am so grateful that I have two good friends from high school to this day: Megs and Alysha. They are still my rock. They never judged me and could handle my outgoing yet insecure self.

It honestly pains me, even now, to think that all the name-calling and empty threats, purely because of how I looked and the gender with whom I felt comfortable socialising, COULD HAVE DESTROYED ME. Their agenda was never transparent; they just hated me.

I wish I could go back in time to my then self, with a bit more life experience, and reassure her, 'It's not you; it's them.' That their life probably sucked, and they needed to bring you down to their level. But I was young, and by this stage, in my middle teens, I had fallen into the dark world of depression, and in turn, I became rebellious.

I became so headstrong and defiant that I turned against the one person who helped me the most: my dear dad. I believe this is because he'd built such a tough exterior with me that we became too alike and clashed.

I hated his authority when all he was trying to do was be the best dad possible.

I'd complain about going to school, and he'd respond with, "Cayle. School is the best years of your life!" At thirty-two years old, he was right, and his words of wisdom didn't stop there. I had many of his philosophical sayings drummed into me. "Cayle, you do as I say, not as I do," and "Not while you're living under my roof." I used to believe my dad hated me. Being a parent now, I completely understand what he was doing.

The constant bullying and my own negative views of my appearance made me feel worthless. I questioned, 'What is even the point of being here?' So many people don't like me. I'm causing my parents so much heartache that dad actually looked into how much boarding school would cost; I was that bad. I just felt like utter garbage. My mindset was so negative. My view on life sucked; I felt like the world was against me, and I should do everyone a favour and give up!

Thankfully, there was something inside me: a voice, a feeling, almost like a fire in my soul, that was planted from a young age. It said: 'DON'T. GIVE. UP. CAYLE!' And so, I didn't; and I am so thankful I saw this through.

Admittedly, deep down, I was probably so stubborn and determined that I wanted to see this through and not let others beat me, bring me down, and ruin me forever.

I strongly believe people who are unhappy with themselves have either had no guidance or direction from their parents or are simply jealous of you (and they will always try and bring you down to their pathetic level). It makes them feel better, right? They've got the company they need down in their miserable holes. Reminiscing on my life's events while writing this chapter, I had focused on who these individuals were, where they came from, and where they are now. The sarcastic devil inside of me had a giggle as I heard The Karma Train stop outside their houses and push them onboard. None of them are as successful as me. None of them have what I have. Sadly, NONE of them had a father like mine.

So, what got me through? My mum, Evelyn. She's a kind soul—the Mother Theresa of our family—who always puts others before herself. She would console me, wipe my tears, and promise everything would be okay. But my dad—the man with the driest sense of humour I've ever come across—did something radically different. Maybe it was the fact that he copped the same kind of bullying as I did because of his name and because he, too, is a short arse. Or maybe, it was the coal mining industry he'd worked for his whole life where everyone had a nickname. *He* was the one who made me tough. *He* made me resilient. *He* made me appreciate the uniqueness of my name, appearance, and the unique personality that grew to match it.

Now, as a mature thirty-two-year-old wife and mother, I can see what my parents did for me, and I am so thankful I came from a good home and had parents who were not willing to give up on me. Throughout those years of being bullied, I learnt the most important lesson of life, which I now instil into my children:

Misery loves company! It thrives like mould in a damp, dark room.

If you are, or were, continuously bullied like me, you quickly notice a pattern with these so-called people. They are folks who are generally unhappy with themselves and their lives, have had no guidance or direction from their parents, or are simply jealous of what and who you are. This was certainly true in my case!

My bullies failed and failed miserably. They never beat me; they actually helped me to some degree. Whether they wanted to or not, they played a role in shaping the person I am today. I like to call it character building.

It became obvious when I started out with my first couple of full-time jobs. My childhood bullying had left a long-term impact on me mentally. My first two jobs were in administration but in an office full of women. I'd drive to work every day feeling anxious, scared of how the day would unfold.

Now, I'm still in administration, coming up on twelve years of service. I bet you've just said to yourself, 'Wow, that's a long time for someone as young as you.' But I'll let you in on a little secret: it's a male-dominated industry.

It was only recently, having kids of my own, that I realised my parents did the best possible job raising me. Given their circumstances, it was a miracle I survived. I'm still a determined b****. Now, my husband says I'm headstrong, stubborn, and often blunt. But this has allowed me to have real relationships where nothing is sugar-coated.

I'm blessed to be a mother to two beautiful children, ages seven and five, one of whom has red hair and freckles. I'm now preparing him for his future. He will already tell anyone that his red hair and freckles are cool! But it's also scary. I am now that mother teaching her children everything she knows about the vicious cycle of bullying. I can teach them, through my experiences, that not everyone in this world is a nice person, and we will often come across people we don't like or people who don't like us; and that's okay! But this does not give anyone the right to put you down and make you feel like how I did all those years ago. Bullying is not okay, and I am so grateful that I am strong enough, like my Dad was, to teach them at a young age—to prepare them the same way he prepared me because I genuinely believe that is what got me through.

I am so proud to stand up and say that I was bullied but never beaten. I will hold my head high knowing that everything that has happened to me made me the woman, wife, and mother I am today!

## BIOGRAPHY

Cayle Lawrence is not only known for being the girl who has a name that no one can pronounce, but she is also a successful business coach and network marketer. She writes in her book about how she was bullied throughout her early years in school and is now using the unique skill set gained from her life's experiences to show others that being determined, resilient, and headstrong will get you wherever you want to be in life. Now, Cayle's mission is to help as many like-minded families escape the rat race of what is perceived as the 'normal life,' to live an abundant life of time and financial freedom so they can spend time with loved ones.

Connect with Cayle Lawrence via https://linktr.ee/Cayle.Ben

CHAPTER 7

# The Extra Mile

*By Chuck Spitzer*

I always thought I was good at what I did. I worked hard and during whatever weird hours needed. I completed the unusual projects that needed completion. I met with the strange, odd customers whom no one else wanted to meet. I covered for those who needed cover. I was that good guy, a handy guy. I say this because I want you to know, in my opinion, I thought I was doing okay.

Then, I got sick. Well, I thought I was just catching a cold. I thought, 'Yep, this is going to be a pain.' But it was worse, **so** much worse. A week later, I was in an ambulance on the way to the hospital! I was coherent, kind of, for a couple of hours. Then, the next six days or so had me in a delirium. I do not recall having any sense of reality during those days, but my wife had some interesting stories about me to tell family and friends. I do have some non-reality stories of my own, but we will save those for when we meet.

Now, those two paragraphs did not seem to be compatible, but stick with me and you will see. When I regained my senses, I found out that I wasn't just sick with a nasty cold; I had pneumonia AND influenza A at the same time, which, by the way, also stopped the function of my kidneys. Now, about a week later, I was leaving the hospital with a walker, a new diet, new medicines, new supplements, on dialysis, and with four days of doctor appointments per week for the foreseeable future. I tell you all this, not for you to feel sorry for me, but to understand why my personal outlook may have been a little bleak.

Now that I was home after a few days, my family began running together as they were all the same. My wife was amazing through all of this. She spent what must have seemed like endless days in the hospital with an apparently hostile patient, followed by caring for me at home. But one thing she did was lead the conversation, and it was positive. We would talk about my time in the hospital, and I gave it exceptional reviews. It was during those times that my perspectives changed. I began to realize that, like my family, the hospital staff, from the aides up through the nurses, took care of me to the best of their abilities!

During my recovery, my family, wife, and sons became my arms and legs for me. With their encouragement and prodding, I worked to wheel myself around, then advanced up to a walker, finally getting back on my own two feet. They would help with my exercises, assist me on walks, and drive me to all my very many appointments. But it wasn't just about recovery. One son became the cook, and my other son became the grocery shopper and personal care helper. They all pitched in to help, but special thanks to my wife.

Now, I know we all like to think that, of course, our family is going to pitch in. But I have seen many that do not. So, over time, I have become incredibly grateful for my family's character. I have witnessed that it is not simply with careers that people excel, but their personal lives. I have personally seen that in any activity, you can excel.

Now, I have been on disability for a while and had to give up my job. So, as I have begun to recover, it was time to look at my future. While I thought I had been good at my previous position, I did not feel fulfilled with that kind of work. I thought about those hospital employees again, my wife's therapy work, and even the selfless help that my family gave me during my recovery, and I felt the need to impact lives. They influenced me by going above and beyond their efforts; they walked the extra mile!

Most people expect and receive the minimum effort from others. But when you get more, it is uncommon. For example, how many waiters and waitresses have you come across in your past? Hundreds? Thousands? Whatever the number, it has been quite a few. But my wife can give you the name of her favorite waitress ever, Michaela. She only ever waited on us a couple of times, and it was over fifteen years ago! But what made her so memorable? The extras! The way she described the foods, glasses were never empty, quick service, the way she prepared the leftovers, and on and on. But her service was above and beyond; she walked the extra mile!

What are the traits or characteristics of impactful people? *Persistent, determined, and decided.* These are words that mean you have made up your mind; this means that what you are doing is in no way uncertain or ambiguous. It is unquestionable and unmistakable. You have unwaveringly decided to do it, whatever it is! The definition of "decide" includes "to cut off." By making the decision "to cut off" any option of failure, you guarantee your impact!

A great example of this kind is a person I know: FR. FR was a child during the depression, and his parents taught him not to waste anything. As he grew up, he became a soldier in WWII. The lessons he picked up throughout his days taught him to take control of his life. He decided that he had to run his own business. He gathered his resources—all his resources—to invest in a business. He investigated available businesses and decided which direction he would go. He made a decision based on a business that would not fail with him. Once he began to gain success, he started to grow his businesses, which grew out to four locations. Then, he started investing in real estate. Then, he added a new business which grew out to two locations. As his businesses grew, so did his investments and success in the community. As his success increased, so did his philanthropy, and he donated to large organizations and individuals in need. His firm will not only kept him on his path to success but evaluated where he could help those around him. I would say he was able to run his extra mile.

*Flexibility and adaptability*, to be able to adjust oneself readily to different conditions. When obstacles get in your way, you figure out how to go over, around, or through them. Non-impactors look at obstacles as the end of the road, and they give up. Impactors see obstacles for what they are: a slow-down to review, a change in plans, or maybe just a recharge. But to the impactor, it is never a reason to quit. It's a reason to improve!

For me, the epitome of adaptability is TS. TS is a physical therapist—easily one of the best out there. But one of her deepest frustrations was that although physical therapy helped many people tremendously, it still had its limitations. So, she did her part to research alternatives and found many ways to treat her patients. Her first alternative was to study a scarcely-known movement therapy for four years. Through her treatments, this method allowed her to achieve great results through different processes and keen observation. By honing her skills into her specialties, she continued to deliver improved results. Being an impactor, TS continued to look for ways to enhance her therapy results. As she tests other complementary therapies, she continues to improve, and proves that she is an extra miler.

*Boldness*, thinking beyond the usual limits of conventional thought or action. Now, I am not saying you must be an Einstein or a Tesla to be an impactor, but do not be afraid of your own ideas. Many of your friends and family will be happy to share their opinions of your ideas, and sadly, a number of you will listen to them. The problem for many of you is that you ignore many experts (who are not your family and friends) willing to help. If your ideas have justified parameters, trust yourself.

RT was bold. She was a high school girls' coach from 1967–1999, basketball first, and later track, cross-country, and softball. But in 1972, Title IX was passed, which opened sports to girls. RT took this as the opportunity it was and became a huge advocate for the girls. She was not a fighter just for girls' sports; she fought to advance her athletes, scholarships, and other opportunities. She battled for girls before other people did. In all, RT-led teams accounted for four state titles, six district championships, two league titles, and twenty-five county championships. The many girls whose lives RT touched would agree that her records were the least of her accolades. They would agree she passed the extra mile.

*Influential and compelling*: these are the bonuses. Do you need these to be an extra miler? No, but maybe you can influence a few more milers. "Compelling" means having a powerful and irresistible effect; requiring acute admiration, attention, or respect. Many milers are compelling and grow to influential positions through their work. They inspire people to do more, some a little, some a lot. Milers inspire many other milers.

KR is my influential miler. He has been a CPA for over thirty-five years. He has worked and climbed his way up to becoming the president and partner of his firm. He has been a board member and president, or chairman of state, for National and International Professional Associations. He has also served on boards and been an officer for several local organizations. As president, he is the company and the voice of the company. His influence has been felt locally and internationally.

*Resolute*, firmly resolved or determined, set in purpose or opinion. I think resolution is the combined sum-total of all the characteristics mentioned above. Some of the synonyms are "relentless," "steadfast," "strong," and "unwavering." A resolute miler will not lose the vision, the purpose of his/her "mileness." The obstacle does not matter as much as the purpose—the purpose is what counts.

All the milers I have chosen until now have been people from my life. But for someone resolute, I have selected a person that most people are probably familiar with, Anthony Robbins. I feel like you will already know anything I say about him. But I will try just a bit. Tony started young by excelling and making others' lives better. He researched until he felt confident he could help others. He then created his vision, his dream. I am sure he modified his plan along the way but kept the vision. Once he started to have his success, his vision continued, making others' lives even better. He started his Meal Programs with Thanksgiving Dinners, and now millions of meals are provided to families every year. Resolute, making others' lives better—his vision.

Now, back to those first two paragraphs. Remember that I thought I was doing okay in my career, but then I got sick. I was forced to start my career over, and I wanted to do better, do more. I decided to watch others to see how they got better. After that, I looked at many people around me to see what made some different from others. Numerous people aren't prudent with their careers or jobs, and some are good like I thought I was.

But there are a few who achieve more—some, so much more! With some extra milers, it was as simple as always doing one thing more than anyone else; for others, it was much more. It doesn't really matter what career you are assessing. There are a few people who are far better than the rest. Why? Because they CHOOSE to be different; they decide to excel.

As I have chosen my new career, my vision is one of an extra miler. My primary goal is to improve other people's lives. My trait of exception is always to do one thing more than other people. But all this was not written to tell you that I have started a new career. I wrote this to explain that you can be exceptional too! You can excel at what you already do or something you want to do. You must decide that that is who you are. You must decide that you do not care if ordinary people will talk about you. You must determine that other people are essential. You must DECIDE! I have found that running the extra mile is a lot less crowded, but the company is great!!

## BIOGRAPHY

Chuck Spitzer has spent years in the training industry. While training in multiple areas like computer skills and soft skills, his favorite years were spent with developing personal skills. Though computer training helped students develop tools they could use for day-to-day tasks, the growth of the individual was significantly more rewarding than the completion of projects. His most cherished days were spent viewing students develop new goals and aspirations that stemmed from entirely new trains of thought.

CHAPTER 8

# Battle With Fear

*By Cyvill May Stewart*

After college, I told my parents that I wanted to work overseas. There were three reasons: better career opportunities, a better quality of life, and adventure. Traveling for the first time feels liberating, scary, and is full of curiosity. You build this perception of what your life will be. The reality won't always follow suit. But it's hard to feel anything but excitement when you have so many possibilities with creating the life you want!

Living abroad shows you how relative the world is. I felt like I was on top of the world for a while, but I didn't live the life I really wanted. Instead, I complied with society's rules. You will experience feelings of being aimless and not fitting in. The truth is we can't run from ourselves. As happy as you may be in a new country, it's natural to wonder if leaving your homeland was the right decision. You miss people. When we decide to move abroad, we do so without any idea for how long!

I planned to stay for a couple of years but ended up staying longer than expected. Even though my life seemed picture-perfect, it was intense and challenging in many ways. I could not handle the many new experiences. It led me to take the focus off other people and look within myself. I did not feel right, deep in my heart and soul. I knew I was called to something completely different. I became restless as this call for something unknown grew more intense by the day. I desperately hoped living someone else's ideal life would be fulfilling. It wasn't. I knew if I didn't make a change right then, life would be the same. You don't change your life; you change your habits. In turn, these habits change your life.

My life wasn't established; I was starting from scratch. Over time, it all seemed monotonous. While work is important, quality of life is even more so. What controls your attention controls your life. Although our careers seem to dominate our lives, it doesn't define who we are. I went from being successful, working in a good position, earning a lot of money, traveling, living my best bachelorette life to living in debts, working three to five jobs, unemployed, broke, and stagnant. The truth is that I struggled to find an authentic path to success for years. But it wasn't too late to change course.

I've been in the corporate world for more than a decade. I worked jobs that didn't always guarantee forty hours a week. I earned just enough to make it through to the next payday, making it difficult to move forward with my goals and dreams. I failed several times, but I did not let that stop me. Life did not change for over a decade, but I was not going to give in to a mediocre future. It was then I told myself enough is enough! Sometimes, to find ourselves, we must lose ourselves, and hitting rock bottom fuels our growth. We're forced to strip away what no longer works for us and build from the ground up. We then become more of who we're meant to be.

What do you think is the biggest obstacle between you and your dreams? Do you think it is the lack of resources, time, or opportunity? Most people do. Here's the truth. The biggest obstacle is something over which you have complete control: FEAR! Your fear influences so much of your life. We can switch our fixed mindset to a growth mindset and use fear as fuel to transform suffering into power. Learning to overcome fear (not getting rid of it because it's something that never goes away) and self-doubt is one of the easiest ways to speed your progress toward a successful life.

I learned more about being myself than I could have ever imagined during those years. I grew in character, developed an independent spirit, and adapted to many new things. Without my experience overseas, I would not be where I am.

The funny thing is that your life becomes what you believe it should be. I believe that I was destined for more. I've been trying to find 'more' for the last ten years, but I know I am paralyzed by fear and holding myself back. Some blocks can completely sabotage your progress and keep you from the results you want. Consider how long you've been feeling the discontentment of not living a fulfilling life. For most people, it has been years. For some, decades. You are the ultimate creator of what happens in your life, be it good or bad. You limit possibilities for yourself based on your results. And your current results have nothing to do with your future. Your current results are evidence of your previous thoughts and beliefs. Let go of your past because the evidence of your future lies in your thoughts of today. Limiting beliefs guarantee limited results.

When you are afraid, you create a mental limit. Beyond this limit, you feel as though you cannot make it, so you don't even try. It shouldn't ever stop you from achieving your dreams. Many people remain where they are because of this fear. The possibility of things going wrong, along with uncertainty, brings in fear. To let go of fear, you have to think about how you can address the worst possible outcome. Once you have a mental plan, you will be able to handle the situation should things go wrong. Don't fill your heart with fear. Rather be thankful you have a chance. Replace self-doubt, believe in yourself, rise above your fears, have faith, and go for it. You will realize you can go further than you think because your limits are way beneath you. Face your fear and take action.

On this path to becoming unstoppable, I had to confront some lingering fears that held me back. Don't wait for the perfect timing; there never will be. Look at your dreams and goals; what is that you really want? What are your passions? Think about them and write them down. Then get them done and be happy! Your intention sets your direction; the outcome you receive is usually the one you expect. If you do not know where you are going, any road will take you there. Do affirmations every day. Surround yourself with people who uplift you. Working three or more jobs doesn't make you any less broke. If I continue exchanging my time for money, I will work the rest of my life, not live it. You deserve a life where weekends and weekdays feel exactly the same. Mindset is everything; it is powerful. It colors every perception. Your mind is like a computer database: if you put in crap, you will get crap. I believe good things come to people who wait, but better things come to those who go out and get them. Many of us might say, "I wish I won the lotto so I become a millionaire." How about we learn a skill, get good at it, and become a millionaire? We haven't the slightest idea of how much we are capable of doing. We are capable of doing anything on which we focus, and we can achieve absolutely anything we want in our lives. One of the most significant determining factors of whether or not our dreams come true is whether we act on them. I know my dreams are bigger than my fears!

Build your confidence and beliefs to help overcome your fears. If you want to build confidence, start by taking action even in the presence of fear. All beliefs are choices, so put away the ones that are limiting. Change your approach and understanding of fear. Fear is usually **F**alse **E**vidence **A**ppearing **R**eal. Check your fears. Are they based on reality? Is it absolutely true? How would you be without this fear? And what if you could transform it into excitement?

From F.E.A.R—False Evidence Appearing Real—to F.E.A.R—Feeling Excited and Ready.

I dream of retiring early and becoming a millionaire because no one in our family has done so. I will be the first one! And I wanted to build a legacy for my children and change the trajectory of what I can achieve. Honestly, I am scared to put it in print. I feel like I could jinx it if I do.

People tell me how lucky I've been to live such an adventurous life. I always say it has nothing to do with luck and everything to do with choosing to work through my fear and following my heart. Our egos are programmed to keep us safe by getting us to play small. I want not just to survive but thrive. This is terrifying for me as my family believes that only hard work equals success. How many people do you know that work so hard but are still unsuccessful? The People close to us are not always going to support us in what we do—DO IT ANYWAY! You are capable of achieving!

Growing up, I was blessed with parents who told me that I could do or be anything I wanted. I truly believe that's the major reason why I've had the courage to work through my fears and live out so many dreams. There will always be people who won't support what we plan to do, be it a friend, a boss, our parents, or a spouse. It is not their life. They have their own. I've disappointed people and even lost a few friends along the way, which was all extremely hard for me. We have only one life, and it is up to live it to the fullest. I would never be satisfied making decisions based on the thoughts and feelings of others. I learned the only way I'll be happy in my life is by living out who I am, following my heart, and embracing the incredible, terrifying, challenging, and awesome life I'm called to live, no matter what anyone thinks.

Fear is a real deal. If you do not feel any fear, then you're doing something. Success is your duty!

THE FEAR. It's real. It sucks on your thoughts, confidence, motivation, and action. In other words, it takes the best of you! We are made for greatness and living our dreams!

And NO, you're not a coward or a weak person for feeling fear. But the question is: Are you *feeling* the fear? Or are you *feeding* it? The former makes you stronger and prepared to move forward. When you open yourself and accept change, you will open the door to many possibilities. You don't need to stay in your situation. And the latter? It results in inaction, low self-confidence, and poor or no results.

While there are more people spending time online, looking for solutions, there are fewer owning up to their shit and upping their game. Most of them are lost in destructions, current circumstances, and stressing over the unknown. To which category do *you* belong? Are you feeling the fear and taking action anyway? Or are you feeding the fear and feeling stuck?

> *"There is so much fear in the land.*
> *You can choose wisdom over fear."*
> —Cyvill May Stewart

## BIOGRAPHY

Cyvill May Stewart is an overseas worker from a small town in the Philippines, now residing in Saskatoon, Saskatchewan. She was a compassionate registered nurse who later in her thirties found passion in becoming a consummate entrepreneur. Cyvill is the mother of two young girls, aged three and one, both smart enough to get the better of her on any given day. She works full-time, navigating the delicate balance between work and family. She enjoys cooking and oil painting. Her book is a great journal of legacy for her princesses, Zoey Alexandra and Meghan Rae. Living abroad had its complexities, but she chose not to be led by fear but through wisdom. She invested in her growth to be better, do better, and have better. Three primary things she stands for are growth, evolving, and thriving. Personal development becomes a daily routine. Update your mindset, update your life. When she gets her tax refund, she invests it in buying all sorts of books.

Connect with Cyvill May Stewart via https://linktr.ee/cyvillstewart

CHAPTER 9

# So, I Failed. So What?!

*By Deborah Clay*

Will this nightmare ever end? That's what I was asking myself as my daughter, my son, and I drove across the country in my 2007 Dodge Caliber filled with what remained of my net worth. I had $1,400 in cash and a few personal items in the hatchback. I was homeless. I could have begged my mom to let me move back home, but I was tired of begging. I was in my fifties, and I needed to stand on my own two feet. I was tired of the rollercoaster of moving back home with mom. Not only was I tired, but I had also made a vow never to move back there, no matter what I had to endure. My mother and I get along best when we have minimal interaction. I didn't want to hear her "I told you so" and "Why don't you get a real job?" I am not the nine-to-five kind of girl.

I was headed for Tennessee. I'd always wanted to visit the South. However, I hadn't anticipated moving to Tennessee because it was to be my last option. I'm a California girl, and I had heard a lot of negative things about the South. I was afraid yet desperate. After all, California is where my family lived. I figured it was Tennessee or Mommy. Tennessee won.

I had put off making a move because I was hoping for a miracle, one that would allow me to stay in California and help me get back into the game of real estate. I had a friend who had moved to Tennessee the year before. She had asked me if I would consider moving there if she bought a house. At the time, I gave her an insincere yes.

Things hadn't been going well in California, and this was around the beginning of the housing crash of 2008. Business was tough, but I was willing to bear it because I was doing what I loved. I'd sold an investment property and made enough money to tide me over for about six months to a year.

So, seizing the opportunity, I buckled down and worked my butt off. I had nine open escrows in a PUD complex. I thought it was the break I needed. 'Once these escrows are closed,' I told myself, 'I'll be fine. I'll get things paid up and still have money left over for a rainy day.'

Unfortunately, that is not what happened. The PUD I had my escrows in were all manufactured homes on permanent foundations. Typically, lenders consider manufactured homes on permanent foundations as real property. That was true until the crash of 2008, when lenders decided not to finance that type of transaction.

I was already barely hanging on. So, I lost everything. My house went into foreclosure, and I needed to move out of my place. But I didn't have the money for the first and last month's rent. I didn't have the money for anything. I was so desperate; I applied for welfare. That was the most humiliating experience of my life, especially for $433 and $200 in food stamps. Oh, I did get medical coverage, though!

For once in my life, I could not see a way out. I didn't know what to do. I finally did the unthinkable and applied for a job at a gas station nearby. The owner told me he couldn't hire me because I was overqualified. I begged the man for that $7.50 per hour job, and I got it. But the pay just wasn't enough.

It seemed the harder I tried, the further behind I got. Finally, it was time for me to vacate my property, but I had nowhere to go. I knew I was in a dire situation. I have always believed in God, so I prayed. I needed to be out of my house by January 21, 2008. A few days later, a friend called me; she said she knew about a vacant house. The cool thing was that it was around the corner from my current home. I knew it was a gift from God.

I know people have different opinions about belief in God, and that is okay. For me, I have experienced too many things in my life to be a doubter. I believe firmly in a Creator. I know some may agree, some may disagree, and that's okay with me. You're entitled to your opinion, and I'm entitled to mine.

I prayed to God, and I got the house. I had neither money for utilities nor the first and last month's rent. But the kind owners let me move in without any money and let me pay what I could until I got on my feet. I will always be grateful to them for their generosity. I was able to move into the house on January 19, 2008. I thought it was the beginning of my recovery. God, however, had a different plan for me.

I knew I still had a lot to learn. I had been living a pretty carefree life, always managing to get what I wanted. Looking back, I took a lot of things for granted in my life. I took my friends, family, and even my God for granted. I was arrogant and self-reliant; I thought I had all the answers.

What I mean to say is that my parents weren't wealthy, but we never had to suffer as kids. We pretty much had whatever we wanted. I would say my parents had six spoiled kids. My siblings realized this flaw in themselves and took precautions that benefit them to this day. I, however, always felt entitled.

I am the oldest of the six, and I took many things for granted. My mom and dad worked and left me to run the house while they were out. I had a lot of responsibility growing up, which, if you're the eldest, you can probably relate to. When mom and dad were out working or away from home, I was the law as far as my siblings were concerned. That taught me how to rely on myself and develop a dislike of being told what to do.

In hindsight, I realize I had to experience the ramifications of the 2008 crash because I needed to be refined. I needed to grow up and learn what it meant to count my blessings. I fell to the bottom of the pit and, though I don't like to admit it, there were times when I considered taking the easy way out. When those times came, I learned to pray before acting, and there were many times when prayer saved my life.

When I moved to Tennessee in 2008, life wasn't easy to begin with. I felt as if I had gone from the frying pan into the fire. However, my time in Tennessee was memorable in that I saw God's hand in my life; I saw how He cared for me in times of trouble.

Looking back, I moved to Tennessee because I was afraid of being homeless. When we arrived in Tennessee, my friend had everything ready for us. We had beautiful, nicely decorated rooms. She had all the accommodations and told me not to worry about anything. She said I would have a job within a month because Tennessee was hot!

I was okay with looking for a job. At the time, I was tired of the ups and downs of real estate, and the market was still a mess. My friend was right. I arrived in Tennessee on July 10, 2008, and I got a job within a month. I was very excited. Things went well until October of 2008, when a competitor sued my friend's employer.

Things became really tough then. However, I found it was easier to face situations with a good friend or a spouse alongside you. My friend went through depression and denial. She didn't have a job and, like me, she wanted a specific type of job. She held out as long as she could but finally had to resort to doing clerical work. At least it helped pay the bills.

I lived in Tennessee from 2008 to 2013. There were ups and downs along the way. However, during that time, I learned a lot. For instance, I realized I am good enough. I now know it's okay to be scared and to use my fear to achieve something worthwhile. I also learned to be willing to go beyond my comfort zone.

Most of all, I learned that God listens to worthwhile prayers and answers them according to His will. I know praying works. When I pray, I feel calm and able to tackle another day. I learned that the caliber of the day I experience is up to me.

Enough about the past. What is my life like today? I got remarried to a wonderful man. By the way, I prayed for the man I wanted, and God sent him to me. I joke with my friends that just as Jehovah called the Israelites out of Egypt, my true love called me out of Tennessee. I moved back to California and am back working in real estate. I have reestablished my credit. My husband and I now own a couple of properties. My son is all grown-up and stays in Tennessee, where he lives with the love of his life.

Life is full of ups and downs. I have learned to be thankful to Jehovah for all the beautiful things He has provided for me. I remember being so depressed that I considered doing something stupid to myself. Now, I'm so glad I looked to a higher source for comfort in my time of need. I shudder to think of the alternative.

Had I chosen to end my life back then, I would have missed out on so many blessings. I am no longer afraid to live, and I have learned that failing is okay. When it happened to me, I chose to get up. I am happy in my sixties, and I am learning to keep turning the pages of my life. I've learned to love living, regardless of what each day brings. Have you done your best and still think you've failed? Then get up, pray, and try again.

## BIOGRAPHY

Deborah Clay is known for her dedication as a Christian Witness of Jehovah. Her mantra, "The righteous one may fall seven times, and he will get up again" (Proverbs 24:16), has been foundational on her road to success. She believes that success is rooted in applying biblical principles to your life. Her mission is to help those who struggle financially and spiritually to change their lives by laying a spiritually solid foundation, then adding secular components to achieve their idea of success.

Connect with Deborah Clay via https://linktr.ee/DeborahC63

CHAPTER 10

# Self-Discipline Through Internal And External Focus

*By Derrick Wilson*

Using the word "Discipline" makes me think of, and relate to, control over one's lives and actions. Discipline can be related to regulation and how we control things from physical, mental, social, and moral aspects of our lives.

We now look at the term "Self-Discipline." To me, the "self" centers and sharpens the focus of the discipline that we should be learning to flawlessly execute in our daily lives. This can include any activity from making a business presentation at work all the way to practicing to become a world-class athlete. In my work life, I administer all types of anesthesia to patients undergoing both surgical and non-surgical procedures. There is a great deal of mental preparation studying the patient or any test results that may have been conducted. From there comes the physical part of the anesthesia administration, followed by preparing the patient for the anesthetic. This is the point where mental preparation meets physical coordination. When I workout, I start with mental preparation and then execute the physical plan I mentally prepared.

Internal focus is where the attention is attracted to the part of the body in question. External focus relates to motor learning by drawing attention to the results of the movement and not the movement itself.

A self-disciplined mind will be better able to bring about the changes necessary for super-performing all daily tasks.

The ultimate goal is to get the physical movement you have created in your mind's internal focus outside the body. This is when internal focus presents itself. As the physical movement begins to occur, your attention changes. At this time, your brain suddenly becomes focused on what is occurring externally. You now become aware of what is going on around you, and you are able to see how well your internal focus planned this physical presentation. The external focus will consist of the planned movement along with the dynamic surrounding environment and any feedback to that movement.

One must close the gap of performance by transferring energy into focused action. No matter your areas of expertise, each of us must capitalize on internal and external focus, both physically and mentally. Whether you are building a house, performing intricate surgery, playing sports, presenting a business plan, or rehabbing an injured body part, internal focus and achievement will play an integral role in how well a task is carried out. You must build on the fundamentals of internal focus and gradually build up to a level of expertise where you consistently hit the mark or go beyond your performance each day.

Internal focus is related to the cognizant thought process of physical performance, where the end results of performance originate in perfecting the thought processes in the brain. Although you will be focused on the body's external physical movements, it will require a great amount of discipline to initiate and forge through the process at a reasonable speed and efficiency. After reaching full speed and efficiency, you must continually evaluate and maintain the discipline to perform better next time.

When you utilize extreme internal focus, you start by programming and visualizing the action in your brain. For example: when you lift weights, you start by thinking of the proper grip, movement, load, and then finally, firing each muscle fiber. You must be able to see the contraction all the way through. You will concentrate on the pattern of each movement and focus on carrying it out each time. If you are giving a business presentation, the internal focus is the same. It may not be as physically demanding or stressful as physical exercise, but the internal focus remains unchanged.

The flow state of the brain utilizing internal focus is an ongoing process. The internal focus must constantly adjust to the sum of the external. There is typically no straight path to the end result. The internal focus must be continuously adjusted and regulated. As your focus goes internally, you are silently talking to yourself as the brain goes through the process of developing the memory to carry out external movements. The height of the thought process is brought about when you are at the pinnacle of internal focus.

The moment internal focus exits the body and is put into motion, it stops, and external focus takes over. External focus involves not only physical movement but other factors as well. These factors are the surroundings present as the movement follows through. External focus gives you feedback on the efficiency of your original internal focus. It may also allow you brief moments of reentering internal focus to make adjustments. Take, for example, a batter trying to hit a baseball that is being hurled to the plate at over 90 mph. The batter starts by positioning himself next to the home plate. He starts internally focusing on how to hit the ball. He will internally focus on the precise pattern to line up and plant his feet in the batter's box. The batter will follow internally by deeply thinking through the flow state of turning their hips inward toward the catcher and holding the bat with the perfect grip strength and angle, with the torso slightly twisted toward the catcher as well. The key is to have all of the coordinates ready to unleash a powerful swing to make contact with that baseball.

Once the pitcher releases the ball to the home plate, the batter's revved-up internal focus processes the pitch to see if he should swing at the ball or not. Once his internal focus gives the green light to make the decision to unload the previously patterned forces, internal focus stops, and external focus quickly emerges with the batter's torso and hips rapidly twisting back toward the pitcher. A powerful, level swing follows this as the eyes maintain a laser focus on the ball.

External focus breaks out with rapid movement to hit the pitch, and all the while, the batter becomes aware of the surroundings involved in ball movement and its hopeful connection with the bat. The surroundings could also consist of the pitcher's movement, breaking of the ball, and the rapid torque of the body and swing. Once the commitment is made to swing, you can no longer internally focus for that brief moment. You are always either internally focusing or externally focusing. Your mind doesn't allow you to do both simultaneously. However, your mind will permit you to go in and out as often as needed in order to make necessary adjustments. This is best illustrated when you see world-class athletes toggle between internal and external focus. They are able to process their surroundings with external focus and make rapid adjustments by going back into internal focus and changing the presentation of external focus. Individuals who become highly disciplined with these focusing techniques are able to transition from internal to external focus seamlessly.

Being able to perfect your internal and external focus requires a high level of self-discipline. I began to practice honing a higher level of self-discipline approximately fifteen years ago. I very much enjoy working as a nurse anesthetist. I began to realize that I would need to become highly disciplined on a daily basis to maintain the level of care I was giving my patients. I wanted to become a more well-rounded anesthetist where I could comfortably take care of all their needs and comorbidities while they were under my care. I wanted to manage each anesthetic with the utmost care. I enjoy the minute-to-minute, sometimes second-to-second, rhythm of the anesthesia and progression of the surgical process. I have been able to maintain weekly studies of anesthesia and continued educational units to maintain my certifications. I have been fortunate to attend and learn at numerous seminars. Ten years ago, I began working at a trauma hospital to learn more about trauma patients, their anesthetic needs, as well as the patients that required a higher acuity of care. Administering an anesthetic requires both intrinsic and extrinsic focus. In your mind, you commit to adjusting the anesthetic according to the vital signs and surgical conditions. It is always a dynamic process.

Practicing the fine art of anesthesia and taking care of patients each day allowed me to focus on my intrinsic and extrinsic processes. I want to continue studying and performing these functions at the highest level, always to be the best that I can be with the patient in the forefront. Many things go on in the operating room simultaneously. It is up to me to maintain the vigilance and dynamic focus of taking care of the patient minute to minute.

As you go about your personal or work life, consider how well you focus on your intrinsic and extrinsic capabilities. Strive to hone these actions so they become flawlessly executed habits without conscious effort. Continually evaluate how you can narrow the focus even further where there is no wasted movement or thought process. Charles Duhigg, in his book, *The Power of Habit,* writes on neuroscience and the understanding of the brain. His writing takes a look at habits and how they operate in a different part of the brain. Use of this area, the *basal ganglia*, does not require a conscious effort. This area of the brain also deals with emotions and voluntary motor functions of the body.

The act of conscious decision-making comes from the *prefrontal cortex*. Internalizing and continually habituating our movements will altogether skip our decision-making mind, and those actions become ingrained. This will create drastic improvements in both the speed and efficiency of that movement. Constantly evaluating the repetition of an action is the key. Always start with the small stuff; these are the fundamentals that should be perfected prior to adding more complex thoughts and movements. As you increase the complexity of the movement and increase repetitions toward perfection, always treat each repetition as if you were performing in the Super Bowl. Whatever you do, learn to climb and master each building block prior to moving to the next level. Remember always to reevaluate, adjust, and improve each step as you execute your performance.

# BIOGRAPHY

Derrick Wilson has been a nurse anesthetist for more than thirty years. In his many hours spent in the fast-paced and tedious world of the operating room, he has always worked to make the flow of anesthesia and surgery more efficient by keeping his primary focus on excellent patient care. He stays on top of new techniques through study and seminars. Derrick Wilson has been an active member of the American Association of Nurse Anesthetists throughout his career. He enjoys working to continuously evaluate and flawlessly execute the safe administration of anesthesia for a higher quality of patient care.

Connect with Derrick Wilson via https://linktr.ee/derrick.wilson

CHAPTER 11

# The Monster In My Bed

*By Doreen Stroud*

It turned out that I was the monster. I had no idea in which direction my life was headed, but I knew one thing: it wasn't good, and it wasn't happy. Reality was slipping.

I don't know when it happened, and I think I have had it for a lot longer than my diagnosis. You've heard of Lupus, but have you ever heard of Lupus psychosis? Neither have I.

I was happily married with three beautiful daughters, and as I look back today and reflect on the last thirty years or so, I wonder about my mental health. I am fifty-eight now and happier than I can remember, except for the day I got married and the day each of my children was born. Getting married and having a family are some of the happiest times in my life. You never think, in twenty-five years, you're going to get sick and get a revolving door in the ER. Carve my name on the revolving door to the hospital because that was my life. That's not something I planned on, but it happened to me.

Let me tell you my story. Once upon a time, I was happy, working in a large, national insurance company. I was so proud of myself. This was my first nine-to-five office job. I was forty-two years old and just started what I thought was a successful career. About five years in, I sought a promotion. I needed to do some studying and learning on my own time. I managed to pass a few modules, but the unexpected happened. Six and a half years of working for them, I got sick. One of the options was to go on short-term disability, get healthy, come back to work, and continue. In the real world, that happens, but it didn't happen that way in my real-world nightmare.

I sprained my ankle, not too severely, but I ended up with a blood clot in my calf. The doctors thought that was a bit unusual, but the worst was yet to come.

I started on a depression spiral. I landed in the hospital's psych ward with severe depression. While I was there, I engaged in some self-harm. I found things around my room to cut my arms and my body. I wasn't trying to commit suicide, but this was my way of coping with the mess in my brain. I had trouble walking; I had difficulty maintaining my balance, and my strength was gone. I was a fifty-year-old using a walker. How debilitating is that? From being very active, running, walking, bike riding, playing sports, playing soccer with my children, to abruptly using a walker. Again, my mental health took a hit. I was incapable of doing anything right ever again. I told myself: 'I am useless. I am broken.'

I engaged in more and more self-harm at home. I was embarrassed, but did not know how to stop. I was crying out for help, but not in the right ways. This was the only way I thought I could stop the nightmare in my head and my body.

I was discharged after about a month and put on anti-depressants that didn't seem to work. The first year, I was in the psych ward three times, anywhere from one-month to three-month stays. The following year, more and more hospitalizations followed. I might as well have put in a revolving door with my name on it. Not only was the psych ward a second home, so was the emergency department. During this stage in my health journey, my immune system went all wonky. I was breaking out in hives and swelling up, yet I was not allergic to anything. I would eat the same food repeatedly, yet I would sometimes end up in the emergency room with severe hives. Sometimes, I would eat the same thing, and nothing would happen. Then, I'd drink a glass of water and break out in hives. What the heck was happening? Another year of questions, another year of depression, another year of the psych ward. This time, I had fluid in my lungs; I was on oxygen. The specialists couldn't find out why the fluid was there, but it was not pneumonia.

Around year three of my nightmare, I ended up with blood clots in my lungs. I remember bits and pieces of what was happening; I remember the call "Code Blue," and that call was for me. I wasn't dead yet. Was I getting ready to die? I recall being unable to catch my breath; I remember struggling for air; I remember the oxygen mask. That's the last memory I have. Several hours passed, and I woke up in the ICU.

Finally, after about ten days, my lungs started to clear, and I was now a guest of the step-down unit for another three weeks. In less than two months, I was back on the same boat: back in the ICU with blood clots, back on oxygen, and struggling to breathe. Prednisone became the drug of choice. A respirologist came to see me and tried to figure out what was going on. She took a biopsy of my lung. Well, that created a new set of problems. My left lung had been deflated, so learning to breathe deeply again was a nightmare in itself. I think I was in the hospital again for about three weeks. My husband came to see me faithfully, and I am grateful for him. He brought me my daily coffee, books, news from the outside world. I leaned on him, and he was there.

I have little to no memory of all these hospital stays, just snippets of things because the swelling in my body was taking over, and the swelling in my brain was hindering any thought process, and memory function was greatly inhibited. My daughters, however, found it stressful to see me in such a state that they chose not to visit. And I don't blame them. It was a terrifying time. They were still young and impressionable.

Around this time of my nightmarish journey, I was finally referred to a rheumatologist, who came back with the diagnosis of Lupus. Well, that was such a relief to put a name on my body turning into a monster. What did we need to do to get my body back on track? Years of medications, years of prednisone, more emergency visits, and hospital stays, but the diagnosis of Lupus did not answer what was happening in my brain. I don't know how many more psyche ward visits I had, but it was more than ten and less than twenty.

I was absolutely bat-shit crazy. My sentences were jumbled. If you attempted to converse with me, I would have sounded like ET trying to talk. What I was saying made sense in my head, but others heard disjointed and stuttering, and sentences making no sense. To the outside world, it was gibberish. I would be very forgetful. I was argumentative. I lashed out at people, especially my family, which to this day, I regret. I have no memory of these actions, only what people have recently told me. My daughters have no relationship with me because of my illness. I know my mental health took a huge toll on my marriage and relationship with my children. I have almost no memory of the next couple of years, except that everything was going to hell in a handbasket. I was acting like a person with OCD but never really diagnosed with a severe case. We all have a few OCD-like tendencies, and that might be a good thing for survival. But what the heck was I doing at 2 a.m., scrubbing behind the fridge and stove? And other strange behaviors.

I realized somewhere along my journey that my marriage was in trouble. I had been to counseling, therapy, psychiatrists, and psychologists. My minister at church also helped me out. But for my marriage to succeed, I knew I needed my husband on board. Unfortunately, it felt like pulling teeth from a dragon. He dug his heels in and even once said to me, 'They can't fix Lupus in counseling.'

In 2015, I decided to leave my marriage. We both fell out of love with each other, and my mental health had an immensely negative impact on my family. I wanted to just leave for one year, get my head on straight, go to counseling, and hopefully revive a relationship that died. But that didn't work out for many reasons. I wallowed in anger, resentment, and self-pity. He wasn't ready to take me back. We both realized it was over.

If it wasn't for my oldest daughter and son-in-law suggesting that we should rent a house together, I don't know where I would have ended up. Looking back, I could have ended up in a shelter somewhere, or worse. I am so grateful my daughter was there for me. I lived with them for about five years, and while I was there, my health began to improve. My mental health started improving as well. I think I might have had two hospital visits, but nothing so drastic as being in the psych ward. Just some Lupus flare-ups put me in the emergency room.

In 2018, my rheumatologist declared that I had something rare: Lupus psychosis. So that's why I felt like I was going crazy. I had no control of what my brain was doing or not doing. It felt good to hear that, but there is little research on what Lupus psychosis actually is. Maybe I'll write a book about it someday.

Lupus psychosis mimics many illnesses, that's why it can take years for a diagnosis. Lupus causes inflammation all over but rarely to the brain. Doctors believe that lupus damages the structures of the nervous system in several ways. It can create antibodies that bind to the nerve cells, which keeps these cells from working correctly. In other cases, lupus antibodies attack the blood vessels that feed nerves, causing the nerves to malfunction. People who often experience mental health issues, MRI scans tend to show that the brain's gray matter has been damaged by lupus.

I started meditating regularly. I started reading again for enjoyment. I was still using a walker to get around but was able to drive, so I had some freedom.

In the summer of 2019, I made some giant leaps. I had weaned off prednisone. I was a bit more active. I was going camping with my daughter and friends. I visited Las Vegas with my best friend. But I still was struggling financially. I was receiving a part of my pension from Canada Pension Plan and spousal support, so I was just okay. But, I could never find a job that would work around my health. I could never go back to an office job. I could not see myself working in a grocery store or big box store because that means standing for a long time. I have muscle aches, weakness in my legs, severe pain, but I will not let that stop me anymore.

I decided to stop using my walker. I started walking using a cane because I still had knee and ankle troubles. But, to be free of a walker was life-changing.

My friend introduced me to this wonderful company called World Financial Group (WFG), wherein I found my purpose. Every week, during training, we focus on personal growth, mentorship, and how to be a leader. We learn about higher law and how it helps in personal growth. We discover how to be challenged in a good way. We are taught how to follow a daily plan and read good books. For example, I'm reading *Atomic Habits* by James Clear right now.

When COVID-19 happened, I knew I was going to be okay. My company pivoted, and I moved with them. We figured how to work online and our product providers have made the leap with us. We have online presentations and run training appointments from home. I will never be out of a job. I will have a career here. I will become successful here.

I bought my first car, by myself, for myself at the ripe old age of 57. I finally found the courage to move out on my own. I am financially independent. I am confident and happy. I have gained so many new friends. I am growing into a leader. I am learning how to mentor others using the training I have received.

WFG changed my life, and I see so much more. I see a future for myself wherein I help others navigate through a debilitating diagnosis, and I teach them how to rise above a severe breakdown. I am an advocate of helping people get insurance on themselves, even if they had been told they were uninsurable. If I was able to get back up one more time, you can too.

Whenever I meditate and write my goals and affirmations, I write that I am connecting with my daughters. I must have faith that I will have a relationship with them, and if it doesn't happen, I have to be okay with that. Staying positive and grateful is important for my mental health. I see the power of asking the Universe to bring unexpected opportunities. It works.

Recently, it has come to my attention that I have said some things that have hurt the people I love. The damage to my brain from Lupus psychosis and two concussions have damaged my "filter". I speak before I think, I react without pausing to think how my words might hurt the people I love. I am trying to make amends, and learning how to put things in place to help censor and help me not blurt out something in frustration.

I hurt the ones I love, and I am trying to make amends. Hopefully this book is an olive branch, a way to reach out to the people I love.

I have gone from a broken, damaged woman to a beautiful, strong, and confident butterfly. If my message has helped one person on this earth, then my struggle has been worth it.

There is no longer a monster in my bed.

## BIOGRAPHY

At the age of fifty-seven, Doreen decided that her life had to move in a new direction or die. She works from home, not as an author but as a budding entrepreneur. She went through years of health setbacks and life-altering illnesses, including one so rare, there is little to no research on it. The chances of having this rare manifestation are approximately .01%, yet recovery is almost 99%. Having lived through a diagnosis of Lupus with a manifestation of Lupus psychosis, Doreen is well-equipped to help people understand and overcome the stigma of a devastating mental and physical illness, which is still a big part of her life, but it does not control her anymore.

Connect with Doreen Stroud via https://linktr.ee/DoreenStr

CHAPTER 12

# Comradery Over Intimidation: Building Teams Because Things Can Always Be Worse

*By Eric Stiles*

Raised on a farm in western Pennsylvania, I grew up going full throttle at all times, regularly experiencing extreme events. The counseling I received consistently amounted to: 'It can always be worse.' And usually, it was.

The first incident I recall was before we moved to our farm. We lived in Akron, Ohio, where my mother and I were trapped in the race riots. We were alone in our car; I was just a little seven-year-old. The terrorists had stopped traffic and were flipping over vehicles and tossing firebombs. My mother told me, "Get Daddy's pistol out of the glove compartment." I did and handed it to her as a mob approached us, breaking car windows and dragging people out of their cars.

She fired several warning shots and slowed the threat. "See if there are any more bullets," she calmly told me. There were two more magazines, so I gave them to her. In a short time, some Army jeeps pulled up and dispersed the mob with some small arms fire and a few .30 caliber machine-gun bursts.

The troops in jeeps spoke to my mother a bit and advised her which direction to escape. She was twenty-eight or so, blonde, with a good figure. So those guys were very helpful.

I'll never forget one of the jeep drivers with a cigarette dangling from his grinning mouth. "Put that gun away now, sonny. You'll get your chance. It can always be worse!" he said with a wink.

As we neared home, I asked my mother, "Can I be an Army man when I grow up?"

"Sure, you can. Not sure Daddy would approve." During that time, my father served as a Marine in Vietnam. As soon as my father returned a few months later, we moved to our farm in the mountains of western Pennsylvania.

We carved out a functional business from the steep, wet, and rocky terrain. The winters were brutal, leaving us snowbound and without electricity for long periods. 'It can always be worse,' I remember wondering for the first time. Okay, this is our attitude, but what is the solution?

In 1972, Hurricane Agnes hit the area hard, pretty much destroying everything we had built so far. "It can always be worse," my father quipped as we removed the rotting corpses of our drowned livestock from the barn wreckage. "Just think, in Cambodia, right now, all this would be dead people. Smells about the same." I remember wondering again about the solution to recover and witnessed that the answer was teamwork. Voluntary teamwork.

In 1973 we enjoyed the Arab Oil Embargo. "It can always be worse," and it was. My mother suffered a stroke that paralyzed her left side. Again, voluntary teamwork and community support made things better. She hasn't had the use of her left arm ever since and suffers a permanent Captain Ahab limp. Talk about a tough lady; she'll tell you that it can always be worse to this day.

The Johnstown flood of 1977 came and went, once more destroying just about everything everyone in the area had built and killing more than eighty people. It can always be worse. I vigorously participated in recovery efforts by building and leading teams. The way we teamed up just made sense (common goals were crystal clear), and I observed how teamwork materializes. Back then, in that area, emergency personnel were volunteers. Again, voluntary teamwork and community support made things better.

During my mid to late teens, I put together teams for projects such as building barns, silos, fencing, harvesting, storing crops, and overhauling machinery. I quickly realized that when people worked together, they produced more efficiently, enjoyed the teamwork, learned from each other, and formed personal bonds based on group success and actual fun. "It can always be worse" helped when things became difficult.

In 1980, many farmers lost everything due to two years of bad weather and a faltering economy. Our farm was one of them. The Selective Service was reinstated, and it looked like we were going to war with Iran. Most of my friends were in their early thirties, served in Vietnam. They all had scars and wounds that were quite bad. To a man, they suggested that guys my age should join the service before getting drafted so we could pick a job that would be less dangerous and provide a trade later on. Because it certainly could always be worse.

I joined the Army because they had the best job selection, and they said I would go to Hawaii for four years. So, I enlisted to be a boat mechanic. Yes, a boat mechanic. In the Army. Army ships remain an unknown asset to this day.

I thought this would teach me super-organized teamwork. Wow. I was in for a surprise.

I found that the leadership and teamwork I initially experienced in the Army were based on threat, coercion, and intimidation. So, I took it. Everyone else did as well because it could be worse.

When I got to my boat mechanic training in Virginia, I found that the others in my group were pretty sharp and friendly fellows who were all already pretty good scientists, electricians, and mechanics. We all had a common goal: complete our school and go to work, all the while demonstrating to our overlords that we could take anything they could dish out. And dish out, they did. It could always be worse.

We had a class leader who wore the red airborne beret, a Vietnam combat patch, and a Combat Infantry Badge. He was very kind to us and showed us how to enjoy working hard. He helped us form into a tight team, and we won all contests and successfully overcame challenges while continuously learning from each other.

I remember feeling that this was the way teamwork should be done. We were so tight that I did some stupid things without giving them a second thought because I had become a super brilliant tech and a physical animal. It could always be worse. So, I made it worse.

We had a classroom instruction about fuel pumps. Fairly simple. But the instructor could barely read. He was pathetic, and everyone was giggling. Eventually, we had to fill out a critique, so I suggested that we no longer be subject to endure illiterate instructors who were unfamiliar with the subject. Things became worse.

Our class received plenty of physical torture with the intent of getting someone to confess. When we got a break, I went to our class leader and told him that I wrote the offending critique. "I know that, Eric. Nobody cares more about getting everything right than you. Because to you, it's instinctive to correct problems before they cause more problems and things get worse, right?"

"But everyone is suffering because of me."

"Shut your mouth and learn your lesson. Nobody will rat you out. That would make our team weaker. Learn your lesson," said our class leader.

I'm sure the cadre figured out that I was the one, but nobody ratted, and eventually, they got tired of torturing us because we took it all with a smile. It could always be worse.

I learned that lesson so hard and well that I did another stupid thing as my pendulum swung the other way. The class leader recommended to the commander that I should attend USMAPS: a prep school with the opportunity to attend West Point. I turned it down because I wanted to be with my team. Pretty dumb.

Then our class leader got killed in a motorcycle wreck. It could always be worse.

My first assignment was as an oiler on the Army's biggest ship in Hawaii. My sergeants were angry all the time and seemed to really hate all new guys. I later found that they were very protective of their positions because they were not very competent at engine room operations. The officers never showed them anything. It could always be worse.

I was cleaning engine parts with a fellow young soldier one day while two sergeants watched. There were some parts that we couldn't quite disassemble right away, and the sergeants laughed at us, called us names, and threatened us.

One of them said, "So you're so stupid that you can't figure that out?"

I looked him square in the eye, fully prepared to take my ass-kicking, punishment, extra duty, whatever. I said, "Yeah, I am. Now, why don't you do your job and show me how?"

Those guys looked at each other, and they never stopped sharing everything they knew with everyone they met. They both became Sergeant Majors, and we are all good friends to this day.

I worked hard and learned harder. I was promoted quickly, sent to many challenging schools, and instructed many of them.

I learned some teambuilding lessons the hard way. That was always because I didn't consult more experienced people first.

We grew the Army's lifelong leadership development program continuously, always working closely with civilian psychology experts. We did so well that we got our NCO Academies accredited through universities.

It could always be worse. The Army had a huge purge in the late 1990s. I was suddenly a civilian. My job paid very well, and the engineering work was familiar. But I noticed that there were no decent teams, and "do what I say, or you're fired" was normal as turnover was high. Nobody was happy or did anything to prevent things from getting worse.

Right away, I was selected to run an expensive, revolutionary, new vessel-type project. I told them something like that would require a team (which nobody in the organization had done)—not a team that operated separately from the rest of the company, but one that would offer participation and opportunity for everyone. They laughed and mentioned that most of the employees were too stupid to understand things like that. That was the heart of their "It could be worse" scenario.

And worse it became. The company went public, and people at and near the top became millionaires. They paid just enough for the ship's crews to keep people from quitting. As people did quit, nobody took their place. Everything was overbudget, and everyone who could steal, embezzle, and pad their expense account did it as hard as they could. No teamwork at all. They were bankrupt within five years.

The greatest team that I ever worked with was on an offshore crane barge with a 275-member crew. We had to make sweeping changes, so we decided to have the entire crew define their specific jobs and procedures in writing. These procedures were converted into safety briefings and permits. This, combined with a generous monthly safety bonus for all, resulted in excellent, safe, and efficient work. The deal was that if there was a single lost-time incident or downtime, absolutely no one would receive their bonus. The people had to watch each other's backs, and everyone is great friends to this day. Suddenly, unreasonable federal regulations crushed this company. It can always be worse.

I worked in several other teams—the best and the worst. The worst was always infected with a toxic, intimidating dictatorship. The best relied upon participative teamwork.

Some of the key points I've come to rely upon are as follows:

1. It can always be worse. We can't predict what's next, but we can always strive to prepare.

2. Teamwork is the answer to most problems. No one can know everything.

3. People instinctively want to be part of groups and teams. Team members should be volunteers.

4. Teams must have common goals among all members.

5. Team members need to share knowledge and skills amongst themselves.

6. A team's members and functioning need to be cohesive but should not be exclusive within the organization.

I don't use the terms 'leader' and 'leadership.' 'Activity Coordinator' is more suitable. 'Leader' is more of a title with today's changing language. It implies superiority over the team.

The activity coordinator must have core competencies, provide direction and resources, and stimulate action through comradery. Things could be worse, and we are all in this together.

The entire organization must be one large team with common goals.

Special project teams should be temporary.

Performance bonuses are the best way to get people to join teams and make them thrive.

Those who threaten and intimidate are rarely successful, and nobody wants to be a part of that team.

It's just my experience. There are many excellent former teammates who say I'm a great leader, and they have me teaching leadership in colleges to this day. I just consider myself a solid, reliable teammate. Because things can always be worse.

## BIOGRAPHY

Eric Stiles is a US Merchant Marine Engineering Officer and Leadership Instructor at Marine Training Institutions around the country. With a lifetime of experience in teambuilding and leadership instruction, Eric has become a sought-after authority on the subject. In this work, his personal worldwide experiences are related to how and why teambuilding works. Mr. Stiles is a US Army veteran. He wrote doctrine and taught Leadership at NCO Academies. He has an MSA in Organizational Administration from Central Michigan University. He has an undergraduate degree from

Saint Leo University in Liberal Arts, and he graduated summa cum laude while on active duty, attending college at night and teaching during the day. Mr. Stiles led many cutting-edge projects in the Southern Hemisphere offshore industry, building a reputation as 'the guy you want to work with.' He lives with his family in Ocala, Florida, where he runs a business and a charity.

Connect with Eric Stiles via https://linktr.ee/enstiles

CHAPTER 13

# Giving Up Is The Only Failure

*By Geoff Cash*

I remember vividly. I was nine years old, and all I wanted for Christmas was the latest gaming system. Christmas Day came, and lo and behold, I GOT the gaming system! I quickly realized the setup didn't include the cables I needed to play because my amazing mother, who was doing her best to provide for me, had spent all her money just buying the system. I was devastated! You see, I grew up with tiny beginnings. I was raised by my amazing grandparents and my mother, who worked hard to support me, although we didn't have much. Little did I know then that the moment when I discovered the missing cables that Christmas Day, along with a few other memorable incidents, would motivate me and give me the drive to succeed. Growing up, seeing my family struggle, and watching my grandfather show me what hard work really is, gave me the FIRE that made me determined I would never again be shorted in life.

By the age of eighteen, I was eager and ready to conquer the world. So, I did what most teenagers do, I enrolled in college. My first major assignment was to write a business plan for a business with revenue of over 350k, but I made a grave mistake that ended my college chapter early; I asked a question. I simply asked my professor, "Have you ever had a business that did 350k in revenue?" He said no. My next comment would be another cornerstone moment in my life: "Then how can you teach me something you haven't done yourself?" I didn't wait for the response; I just packed up my stuff, and that was the end of my college education.

I then entered the working world, where I knew I didn't want to trade time for money, so I started my first business. It was in the financial sector. My grandfather had instilled in me his work ethic, which, he assured me, would catapult me to success levels I didn't even realize existed. With that, it seemed that one day I was living off fifty-cent burritos, to avoid the embarrassment of admitting I had no money, to the next day being able to afford more or less anything I wanted. Life was GREAT! By now, I'm sure you're saying this chapter of the book makes no sense, but don't worry, it's coming. You see, I was so caught up in the trips, the cars, the "lifestyle," as they say, that I wasn't watching my business. The next thing I knew, it was gone. Through one wrong and immature move, I lost it all. All the cars, the trips, the dream house, and the whole lifestyle was suddenly GONE!

That period in my life was really dark. I started out blaming everyone and everything for losing "my life." But it wasn't anyone's fault except my own! I buckled down and started focusing every day on developing myself. Through reading and being around others, I realized I had a choice; I could continue to be sorry for myself, or I could decide not to give up and become great! So, I went straight to work building another company, and when I call it a grind, I worked harder than I had ever worked before.

A few years later, things were looking up once more. I had gone from knocking on doors to traveling all over the country, building my business once again from the ground up. Things were booming, and I thought, I'm back! That's when things started to go south again, mainly because I'd made the mistake of hiring some of the wrong people to work in my company. It turned out that, behind my back, these folks had not been following any of our business principles. Not only were they unethical, but they were outright robbing me! I remember telling my wife our life was about to drastically change. Over the next few months, we went through losing our home, cars, savings, and, eventually, faced bankruptcy. That was my true rock-bottom moment. Losing everything again was hard, but not being able to protect my wife, something I'd vowed to do, was just about destroying me. I frequently asked myself why I should bother to keep trying. I wracked my brains to find a way through the situation. I questioned my ability to provide my wife with the life I had promised her. It felt as if everything was telling me to quit trying for good. But I didn't; through prayer and immersing myself in personal development, I finally decided to keep going because quitting is truly the only failure!

At that moment, a line from a very famous movie, *Rocky*, echoed in my head: "It ain't about how hard you hit, it's about how hard you can get hit and keep moving forward!" With that in mind, I dove headfirst into personal development harder than ever and rebuilt the business.

Going through all that was possibly the hardest thing I've ever experienced. The stress was so great, and it caused so many personal, family, and marriage problems. I felt like giving up again or running away. Heck, I even felt suicidal at times. But I knew there must be others like me out there and that I must help them. Wanting to share my experiences with others for their benefit became the reason for writing this book.

Don't get me wrong if I say to you, I don't care what you're going through right now; maybe your marriage is failing, you've lost your job, a family member has passed, or your beloved pet has died—it doesn't matter what it is, because NONE of these things add up to failure; they're simply opportunities for growth! You only fail if you give up!

I know you're saying, "Geoff, that sounds good and all, but my situation is different. You don't understand; it's just so hard." Look, let me tell you—stop lying to yourself! You'll never accomplish any of your goals in life by lying to yourself. The first step to recovery is making the commitment never to give up. The next step is to list all the reasons why the situation you're in has occurred. When you're making your list, it's important to be as honest with yourself as possible, or it's not worth the ink on the paper. Once you've made your list, the third step is to write down exactly what you've done so far, if anything, to control your current situation. The odds are, you won't find many matches. That means the question to ponder is, if you haven't tried preventing the situation from developing, then why are you moping and complaining about it?

As humans, we're programmed from a very young age to think the world is against us. For instance, when people do well, others often say,

"Oh, they're so lucky!" or "If only I could be that lucky." Hell, you may even have said that yourself! Let me break the news to you: the "lucky" ones are, in fact, the "prepared" ones. The more prepared you are to take on any challenge, the luckier you will find yourself. I'm not going to coddle you here, unlike the rest of the world. You must understand, this business about being lucky is all B.S. Don't believe it!

No matter what situations we face in life, it's the choices we make about those situations which determine the outcomes. Get it out of your head that life is always going to be perfect; it ain't! But as humans, we are powerful beyond measure, and the best news is we have the choice to be great and, more importantly, the choice never to give up!

By now, you're probably saying, "Okay, I made my list; I see I did nothing to prevent the situation from happening. How do I get back up?" Here comes the good part: The HARDEST part is taking the first step; choosing not to give up. You already have what it takes to be great; you just need to choose to be great. Always stand tall, stand proud, and never be ashamed if you fall, because, I say it once again, true failure only comes when you give up!

## BIOGRAPHY

Geoff Cash is a self-made entrepreneur who has built several successful businesses. He comes from very small beginnings but has now been featured in publications such as *NY Weekly, LA Wire, Chicago Journal, US News*, and *American Reporter*, as well as being tagged as a "Future Shark." His visionary leadership has seen him mentor and train thousands of people in sales development. His passions include spending quality time and traveling with his wife and finding time to squeeze in as many rounds of golf as he can. He lives by the motto of doing as much as he can, for as long as he can, to help as many as he can.

Connect with Geoff Cash via http://www.geoffcash.com

CHAPTER 14

# The Center Of Building Your Relationship With Others

*By Henry Atchison*

There are some people in this world who have never met a stranger. Now, this might sound a little funny or hard to believe on the surface. So, what exactly did that statement mean? To put it in simple terms, there are some people who can relate to *anybody* and *everybody* immediately. I am sure you have come across such folks; I know I have.

I worked with a sergeant in the military who was the embodied of such a talent. Sgt. Mulkey and I could go anywhere, and he would be able to strike a conversation with anyone we came across. Having great admiration for such a skill, I tried to build casual relationships with people on various occasions, but it just never seemed to work out for me. What did Sgt. Mulkey have that I lacked? Rapport. Sgt. Mulkey had the natural ability to build rapport with whoever he met. So, what is rapport?

The Merriam-Webster dictionary defines rapport as: "A friendly, harmonious relationship, especially: a relationship characterized by agreement, mutual understanding, or empathy that makes communication possible or easy."[5]

So, how do we, like Sgt. Mulkey, build rapport with strangers? There are several factors that come into play in building rapport.

---

[5] "Rapport," Merriam-Webster (Merriam-Webster), accessed April 25, 2021, https://www.merriam-webster.com/dictionary/rapport.

1. Maintaining a Good Appearance

It is essential that you maintain a presentable outward appearance to create rapport in its initial stages. Your appearance should not be a hurdle when communicating with the other person. The impression you make on others—especially first impressions—is crucial to rapport building.

Here's a helpful tip to keep in mind when you're preparing to get into a meeting: dress in a manner that you feel most people will. Now, if you're afraid of being underdressed or overdressed, pick an outfit that can be easily dressed up or down.

Dressing well and having a presentable appearance are important in establishing rapport with others because taking your appearance seriously shows that you respect yourself and the people around you.

2. Be Open

Being open involves good verbal and body language. Good verbal communication is also an essential part of building rapport, but so is body language. Use both to communicate your openness to the other person. Here are a few ways you can do this:

  a. Maintain a good posture when talking to the other person
  b. If possible, do a bit of background research on them so you can cater a conversation to their liking
  c. Remember their names
  d. Maintain a relaxed mood to put them at ease

Doing this will show them that you are open to conversing and getting to know them, and they will be more likely to open up to you.

3. Be Real

Making a good impression on someone does not mean lying to them. In fact, doing so is more likely to push them away. Nobody likes a hidden agenda. So, in addition to being open, you must also be transparent and authentic in your approach. This is a surefire way of boosting healthy rapport.

4. Find a Common Interest

Finding common interests brings people together. But keep in mind that not everyone will have the same interests as you or even the same attitudes on a shared interest, and this could become a negative link instead of a positive one.

What you can do here is explore the person's viewpoints on various subjects before you share yours so that you can fish out something that strikes a mutual chord. Explore the person's hobbies, travel ideas, sports, or any other interests. Eventually when you both share similar thoughts on a subject, communication will tend to flow smoothly.

5. Be Friendly

If you give a first impression that comes off as proud, arrogant, or egotistical, you will soon find that you will have no one's attention. Maintaining a friendly demeanor is necessary because it creates a lasting impact on the other person.

Some ways you can give off a warm and friendly disposition are smiling, making good eye contact, and stirring up interesting conversations. All of these are routes to building healthy rapport.

6. Be Empathetic

There is a saying, "Never judge someone until you've walked a mile in their shoes." To put it simply, place yourself in the shoes of the other person. Try to think of their needs and wants. Empathy involves recognizing the other person's emotions. However, don't just simply do that; actively listen to what they say. At the same time, be sure to share your views as well. After all, communication is a two-way street.

Empathizing with the other person, active listening, and responding to their views in a friendly manner will boost rapport.

Now that we've touched on the more classic methods of rapport building, we can delve into leveraging rapport for our network marketing business. Keep in mind that the real purpose of rapport is to get people to **know**, **like**, and **trust** you.

You should always strive to show your honesty, integrity, and sincerity to others. It allows them to understand that you have their best interests at heart. Going off about your own agenda does nothing to build rapport.

Think about the last person with whom you had an interaction who did not believe what you had to say. Then, analyze the interaction based on the questions below:

Did you behave honestly with them?

Did you demonstrate your integrity?

Did you show your sincerity?

Did you truly have their best interests at heart?

Perhaps you may have answered 'yes' to all those questions, yet the person did not seem to believe you. You failed to convince them; nothing was accomplished. Why? A positive response to all four of the aforementioned questions is not indicative of building genuine rapport.

Now, think about a con man.

Is the con man honest? No.

Does the con man have integrity? No.

Is the con man sincere? No.

And does the con man have the prospect's best interests at heart? No.

Yet, the con man often creates rapport with people rapidly. He has the ability to convince honest, hard-working people to hand over their money in a matter of minutes.

Honesty, integrity, sincerity, and having your prospect's best interests at heart are very important. But they do not build rapport in themselves. It takes more than just that.

Firstly, if someone does not share the same views with you on a subject matter, they automatically tend to build a wall of disbelief between you and them; skepticism comes to the forefront. Psychologically speaking, we tend to trust people who think like us and see the world from the same point of view. An example will elucidate this.

Let's say you are an American in Japan. You are surrounded by mostly Japanese people. Then, you meet someone from America. Almost immediately, you both build rapport with each other. A bond is formed, and trust is instantaneously established because the other person is more like you than everyone else around you.

Secondly, the way your present yourself to the other person can either build or kill rapport. Here's an example that explains how.

Imagine a Texan goes to New York City to meet a bunch of three-piece-suit-wearing investment bankers. The Texan is dressed in a cowboy hat, jeans, and worn-out boots. He begins the meeting with a slow southern drawl, saying, "Y'all have a seat. I'm fixing to get ready to start this here presentation." How likely is he to make a sale in the scenario? Little to no chance.

Let's take rapport building to the next level. We talked about appearances and sharing the same views. What are some other simple ways you can build rapport?

A simple smile speaks volumes. It is one of the best rapport-building and communication tools. And the best part is that it costs absolutely nothing. Now, I know there are some of us who have not smiled for years. So, it may take some practice to get that going. Think about this. A one-year-old baby can determine if you are safe or dangerous simply by looking at your smile; they may even return it. Not that your prospect is a one-year-old, but the dynamics involved here are the same.

In written communication, make sure you establish rapport with the person using friendly language and various positive emojis (especially the smiling emoji).

One of the most important rapport-building tips is to remember a prospect's name. To take it further, use the prospect's name periodically. If they have an unusual name, a good response that will stir up a friendly conversation might be, "You have an interesting name. I am curious as to the history behind it." Quick side note: in my case, my name was passed from uncle to nephew down the family generations.

Now, we get into the interesting part of rapport-building: what do you talk about? This stuff is so good, it should barely be legal.

1. Tell your prospect **one fact** they can believe.
2. Tell your prospect **another fact** they can believe.
3. Smile.

Here is an example:

1. "Most people want to save money on their taxes."
2. "Most people want to live and stay healthy to enjoy their retirement years."
3. *Smile*

Notice how the two facts begin with 'most people,' and not 'everybody.' That's simply because they don't apply to everyone. Regarding the first face, if someone is living on social security, paying taxes will not apply to them. With the second fact, there are some people who wish to have problems in their retirement years simply so that their grandchildren will come to visit them more often. By saying 'most people' at the beginning of a sentence, your prospect is likely to ask themselves, "Am I a part of the 'most people' or am I one of the few people?"

Other similar phrases that can be used in the beginning of stating facts so that people will interpret them as being true are:

"**Everybody** knows . . ."

If everybody knows it, then it is most likely true.

"**Everybody** says . . ."

If everybody says it, then it is most likely true. "Well, **you know how** . . ."

If I know how, then it is most likely true.

"There is an **old saying** . . ."

If the saying has been around a long time, then it is most likely true.

Sometimes, I combine these phrases in a coherent manner in order to successfully build and maintain rapport with the other person. What I say to them goes along these lines:

"**There is an old saying**, 'If we don't keep our bodies healthy, then we won't live very long.' **But everybody knows** we don't have the time to eat healthily. **Most people** are too busy to take the extra time to exercise regularly. Well, **you know how it is**: we'd certainly take better care of ourselves if it were quick and easy."☺

People are very likely to positively respond to this, unless you give off the salesman vibe. To turn off the 'salesman alarm' and maintain rapport, ask the question:

"Do you know anyone who . . ."

Notice that instead of pitching and presenting to the prospect (and unintentionally coming off as a salesman), you put your prospect in a question-asking mode. It is easy to execute as well as polite. Nobody enjoys a one-way conversation; remember that conversation is always a two-way street. You may even ask the question, "What would you like to know first?" The question you need to avoid is "Why?"

Is it challenging to get people to believe you? No, **everybody knows** it is easy to get people to believe in the true and good things you say.

What about rapport? It can be established very quickly. Within a matter of seconds, the automatic program embedded in people's heads makes a quick decision about whether they want to trust someone or not.

Now that you have the tools to build rapport, put them to use. The rest is up to you.

## BIOGRAPHY

Henry Atchison has been developing computer programs for over fifty years. When honorably discharged from the United States Air Force, he moved to the Dallas area with his wife and two boys. He got a job with a local aircraft manufacturer in the computer department, where he began computer programming. He graduated from UTA with a business degree. He has been in the computer program development profession ever since, working for the Federal Reserve Bank, Frito Lay, Amarillo National Bank, and contract programming at IBM. When the contract expired, he worked for a software development company called Systemware before retiring. Wanting to keep his mind active and to avoid Alzheimer's disease, and with eighty years of life experience, he takes no drugs of any kind and still works with Systemware twenty-four hours a week.

Connect with Henry Atchison via https://linktr.ee/Henry.Atchison

CHAPTER 15

# 9G's To T-10

*By Jack Thomas, Jr.*

I am blessed with many wonderful friends who inspire me with their lives. I enjoy hearing their stories of how they overcame obstacles and turned lemons into lemonade. I do have some of my own to share with you. Life has its many twists and turns: some good and some not so good. Our life is what we make of it. These are some of my experiences.

As a young boy growing up in Central Illinois in a family with five Baptist preachers, I never thought I would have been to the places I've been, seen and done things I have, and not to mention meeting all the people whose paths have crossed mine. I grew up in a blue-collar family with both parents working. My father was a truck driver and worked on the side for my grandparents, laying carpet. My mother was a waitress until they divorced when I was thirteen years old.

**High School**

In 1985, I was in the tenth grade. I transferred schools from Arizona back to my hometown in Illinois. On a March day, I was sitting in English class when I heard a voice over the speaker asking if I was in class. The teacher replied, 'Yes,' and I was instructed to go to the office with my things. When I arrived, the secretary told me to go into the Assistant Principal's office. I entered his office and saw my mother there. I remember asking her, 'What are you doing here?' She didn't get to answer, as the Assistant

Principal rudely told me to sit down. During this meeting with the three of us, I was told to leave the high school and the school district because I had too many credits for being a sophomore. The school told my mother they were taking credits from me: core credits such as math, science, history, and a couple of elective classes. She fought with them tooth and nail and told them they couldn't take credits already earned only to be told: 'We can do whatever we like, and we will.' To be kicked out of the school district meant I would have to go to a school in one of the smaller outlying towns from the city. The cost to go to one of these out-of-district schools at the time was $2500.

A single mother who never received any child support could not afford to send me to an outlying school, let alone a private school in the city. The only alternative for me was to get a GED. My thought at the time was that I'd been robbed of my education. After about a week, I was at the community college signing up to take the GED classes. After talking all this over with my mother and still confused at why all this happened, I didn't let it hold me back. In August 1986, I graduated with my GED. High School was behind me. 'Now, what do I do with my life?' I asked myself.

I started taking college classes. After all the fiasco with high school, I thought I was on my way by attending college. I wasn't ready for college. I left college and went to California to spend time with my father and then to Texas to spend time with family friends. After this short year and a half journey, I again asked myself what I should do with my life. I went to my grandfather and talked to him. He gave me the loving advice and options any grandfather could give to a grandson. The only option I had was to join the military.

**Military Service**

I joined the military at the age of nineteen and served twenty-seven years from 1988 to 2017. In the Army, I was an aircraft power plant repairer. In the Air Force, I was an F-16 Crew Chief/Flight Chief.

The Air Force and its reserve components, the Air National Guard and the Air Force Reserves, significantly impacted my life. One of my most important opportunities in the Air Force was to mentor and train new airmen. Everyone came from all walks of life in the military—different ethnicities, levels of education, and income brackets. Some were ordinary people, and there were others who played professional sports but gave up their mark to serve their country. Here are a couple of things I encountered in the military that were failures to others and me. We learn from our failures to become better people.

1988, while in basic training in the Army, I pushed myself to become strong. I entered basic training, only standing 5'5" tall and weighing 118 pounds. Six months later, when I graduated Advanced Individual Training (AIT), I weighed 135 pounds and could run two miles in ten minutes and forty-three seconds. If you've never gone through military training when in formation, they always put the tall people up front. We short people had to keep up with the garrison with all our gear. I remember we were on a road march, coming back from a range one day. I was carrying a sixty-pound rucksack on my back when I noticed quite a few taller people were falling out because they couldn't make it for whatever reasons. Those who fell out were picked up and rode off in a truck while the rest of us completed the road march. As I walked along, my mind began to race, and I told myself that I could do this. Don't be that guy! You are better than them. They are bigger and stronger than you, but you can show them you are more robust for your body size. Basic military training is physical agility and a mind game. After completing that twenty-mile road march and thinking back on every march we made, I didn't fall out of any. I became more robust every day of training, and I never gave up.

In 2004, while assigned to an Air National Guard F-16 Fighter Wing, we were deployed to Incirlik AB, located in Adana, Turkey, to fly the Northern No-Fly Zone over Iraq. While preparing for the deployment, I had two subordinate airmen directly assigned to me—a Tech Sergeant (TSgt) and an Airman First Class (A1C). For every deployment, there is a specific number of people who go. If one person goes down, their workload carries over to the others. My two subordinates ended up going home just two weeks after being on station in the country. After getting back home from the deployment, we learned why they came back so soon. The Air Force's second core value, "Service Before Self," had been violated by these airmen.

After speaking with them, the A1C and I had to go before the commander. The A1C scored a failing grade on his upgrade test. This meeting turned into more controversy for me than one could imagine. The meeting with the commander led the A1C and the TSgt to write falsified letters to defame me, and I was forced to leave the Air Force against my will. I was threatened with either going out voluntarily or being kicked out with a dishonorable discharge. I knew I did nothing wrong. I was furious and hurt to think the country I loved and protected could do this to me. It took three years to prove I was innocent, and I didn't make the statement they stated in the false letters. It cost me three years of my career.

I almost gave up fighting because of the time it would take. It was my word against two subordinates, a Fighter Wing Commander and his staff of Officers, JAG, and Senior enlisted NCOs. When I asked for a JAG, they said, 'No, hire an attorney.' I'm not a quitter. I did just that, and I won my case because of the core values the Air Force instilled into me: "Integrity First." I reenlisted and went on to finish my military career with twenty-seven years. The three years it took for me to prove I was innocent kept me from reaching thirty years of service. I learned from this incident that I am not a quitter. I think some get lost and forget several things. The first is the core values instilled in us. The second is respecting the rank and its authority. You don't have to like the person, but you have to respect the rank. They didn't respect me, and they failed to respect my rank.

**Military Retirement**

I retired out of the military in October 2017. I was assigned to a reserve unit in Ft. Worth, Texas. I remember the day I sat down with my Chief to talk about my retirement ceremony. I had chosen a Three-Star General, a former Unit Commander, a former Director of the Air National Guard, and a Federal Judge. My Chief would not allow me to have the general retire me out. Why? Because the protocol was completely different from having an officer of lower rank perform the ceremony. I didn't get my ceremony. I didn't get my flag or any of my retirement certificates. I've tried to get these items. I finally gave up in 2020. My country failed me. I still love my country and will serve again if it ever needs me. I learned from this that no matter how much they stomp you to the ground, you must get up, brush yourself off, and smile. It's only pieces of paper. Paper means nothing. I will always have the memories, and I still have my pride and dignity. They'll never take that from me.

**Civilian Work**

I have worked on some great projects, from military to civilian aircraft, and now a space program, throughout my career. I don't know if it is me, or if others may think as I do, but I never thought I could be part of history in the making; but, I am. In 1903, when the Wright Brothers flew the first powered flight at Kitty Hawk, aviation history was born. Technology progressively advanced to get us to the jet age, and Chuck Yeager soared into aviation history in 1947—the first person to break the sound barrier. For me, my history-making came in 2007 when I worked at Eclipse Aviation. In the early to mid-2000s, the race to build and fly the first Very Light Jet (VLJ) was on. There were several companies, but Eclipse became the first of a new class of Very Light Jets when delivered in late 2006. Then in 2009, I worked the Boeing 787 Dreamliner® program. It took to the skies for the first time and launched a new era of aviation. Other programs include the Gulfstream 650®, and those are part of aviation history or will be soon.

Fast forward to 2021. I am now working on a space program. It is exciting to know I am part of something this big. I have been an aircraft mechanic, inspector, Quality Engineer, Director of Maintenance, and

Flight Chief. I am taking my experience from the military and aerospace industry and using it to teach others. Most people chase after their dreams early on in life. For me, now is the time. I have learned so many lessons throughout my career. One of the most valuable skills I learned in the military is to be a mentor. I am taking this skill and using it to help others.

From all the success and failures I have encountered throughout my life, there is one thing that made me who I am today. I always get up, brush myself off, and press on. Watching my mother do the same thing taught me that life could be challenging at times, but you had to press on, no matter the circumstances. My family and my faith in Jesus Christ have got me to where I need to be in life. Life is an exciting journey for me now.

## BIOGRAPHY

Jack Thomas, Jr. grew up in a small Midwest town known for industrial and agricultural commodity processing and production. He joined the military two years after receiving his GED and learned the trade of aircraft maintenance. After a few years in the military and attending other military schools, he realized it was his calling. During his twenty-seven-year career, his leadership motivated the lives of many airmen. To this day, he has remained true to his calling to inspire, mentor and coach others to rise to their highest potential. He is an FAA Certificated Airframe and power plant mechanic and a member of the American Society for Quality and USCCA. He enjoys baseball, hockey, NASCAR, Formula 1 racing, hiking, camping, sport shooting, flying, and spending time with his family and friends.

Connect with Jack Thomas Jr. via https://linktr.ee/jethomasjr

CHAPTER 16

# The Keys To Unlocking Your Prison

*By Jameson Chin*

I believe everyone deserves better. I believe everyone deserves to be loved. And I know that happiness is truly a conscious choice we can make **every single time**.

    I stood there, staring out the window with tears streaming down my face, watching and listening to the raging thunderstorm. It felt as if the heavens knew exactly what was going on and were crying out for me. I had just lost a newfound job I really loved, closed down my business into which I had poured out my heart and soul, and I was stuck in one of the most toxic relationships I've ever had in my entire life. Things were so bad that even the people with whom I hadn't been in contact for years were asking me if I was okay. To top it all off, I hadn't slept properly at all for the last six months.

    That was my lowest point in life, and I even contemplated ending it all.

    But as I stared blankly into space, somehow, I recalled this quote from Justine Okwesili: "The mind is a powerful force. It can enslave us or empower us. It can plunge us into the depths of misery or take us to the height of ecstasy. Learn to use the power wisely."[6]

    And that was my wake-up call.

---

[6] "JUSTINE OKWESILI Quotes," YourQuote, May 15, 2020, https://www.yourquote.in/justine-okwesili-bwhwi/quotes.

Being someone who believes in multiple sources of income, I pounced at the opportunity of starting my own business in the limousine industry. Being a people person, I loved interacting with my clients; the meaningful conversations brought me great joy, especially seeing their satisfaction when they thanked me for my services. That indescribable feeling always felt really good when I knew that I made a difference.

And then, one day, I met Diane (not her real name). She was beautiful, smart, witty, and also an entrepreneur. There was something about her I couldn't explain. She was the kind of person who could complete my sentences and understand my jokes. We got along well; it felt like we'd known each other forever. Eventually, we got together.

In the beginning, things were smooth. We had lots of fun, and I thought we were a great match. But things started to change as I got to know her better over the following months. I began to see another side of her, and the first problem I faced was believing the things she said. There were countless times where I caught her lying (and I'm talking about simple, small things). The dinner she promised to cook never came. The dates we arranged would be postponed. It didn't seem to be such a big deal initially, but she would get upset over why I would question her over such small things when the topic came up. My concern was more about the principle behind it. I firmly believe that how you do *something* is how you do *everything*. Saying something and not doing it reflects badly on a person's credibility. Occasional hiccups are acceptable, but not when it repeats so often that you're dealing with it a few times a week.

The next problem was her drinking habits. She would consume alcohol as if it were water. And when she got drunk, her appetite for alcohol increased. I do not have anything against people who consume alcohol, and in fact, I have many close friends who do so with great control. Most of them are responsible enough to know when to stop, but Diane was the kind who couldn't control herself. I remember a few occasions where she would get so drunk and end up lying on the floor in a pub, and I would have to actually carry her to a taxi to send her home.

Diane became an entirely different person after alcohol touched her lips, and she wasn't a friendly drunk. After drinking, she became an emotional wreck, cried about how horrible her life was and how she wished to end it all. And when she finally got tired, she would cry herself to sleep and wake up the next day regretting the events that had happened, only to repeat this whole cycle again a few days later.

> *"The definition of insanity is doing the same thing over and over again, but expecting different results."*[7]
>
> —Albert Einstein

As time went on, these problems started to grow. I truly believe that one of the pillars of a strong relationship is effective communication. Yet, there were many times when we quarreled, and when I tried to explain my side of the story, she would shout at me and tell me to stop justifying myself. All I would try to do was explain what was happening. She would say things and expect me to "read between the lines" because I was supposed to "understand her." And there were many times I got it wrong. At times, she got physical and hit me, and even threatened to commit suicide. But time after time, I would give in to her and let her have her way because I loved her.

    As the months passed, this dream relationship turned into my worst nightmare. It started taking a toll on my life and my relationships with the people I was closest with. I started becoming distant, cold, and I had trouble sleeping. I had to close down my limousine business because I could no longer connect with people at the level required of me. And because I needed money, I set out to find a job. After much searching, I found one I really liked, but alas, I couldn't keep my job because I was

---

7   Trent Hamm, "If You Want Different Results, You Have to Try Different Approaches," The Simple Dollar, November 11, 2020, https://www.thesimpledollar.com/make-money/if-you-want-different-results-you-have-to-try-different-approaches/#:~:text=Albert%20Einstein%20is%20widely%20credited,%2C%20but%20expecting%20different%20results.%E2%80%9D.

unable to concentrate due to fatigue and stress. I started spiraling down into depression, and there were times I considered ending my life. From the positive person I once was, I became one of the most negative people I'd ever known.

I became the exact person I always told people not to be.

I absolutely hated myself and what I had become. However, I was blessed with family members and friends who kept telling me to seek God for strength and direction and assured me that I could always turn to them whenever needed.

So, as I stood there at the window one night amidst the thunderstorm, I realized that I had to do something about it, or I would forever be stuck in this situation. I started to evaluate myself and my actions, and I started praying to God for guidance.

It was in life's darkest times that I saw the light because it shone the brightest.

After so many months of pain and heartache, I found the problem: ME.

I finally realized that *I* was the **sole reason** I was in that state. And it's because I **allowed** it. Once I came to terms with the fact that I had a choice and a part to play in my own happiness, things started to change. My mentor once told me: "You teach people how to treat you." And my mentor was absolutely right.

*I* allowed ALL of this to happen to me.

Every time she threatened me with suicide, *I* would give in.

Every time she got drunk, *I* would put up with her attitude.

Every time she lied to me, *I* would give her another chance.

Every time she hit me, *I* would just tell myself that she was going through a tough time and that she needed to let off some steam.

The physical, mental, and emotional abuse was something that **I ALLOWED TO HAPPEN TO ME**.

I realized that I didn't love myself enough, that I didn't set any boundaries. That was all I could think about. How much would I end up losing? I couldn't see how much I'd already lost by allowing this to happen.

I'm not saying that you shouldn't have any compassion, nor am I saying that you should take what people say lightly. What I'm saying is that you have to remember that *you* are in control of your own happiness and that *your* happiness shouldn't depend on how others feel. You are the only person in your life who knows *exactly* how you are feeling, and you are the sole person who can *allow yourself* to feel however you want to feel. It is as though you are the prison warden, and you can choose to lock in whatever feelings you want and keep out whatever you don't want. And if you don't want to feel that way, you have **EVERY RIGHT** to remove yourself from that position of weakness, hurt, or pain, and you are allowed to put yourself in a position of **POWER**, **CONTROL**, and **STRENGTH**.

I want you to remember this, and I want you to give yourself the permission to **ALLOW** yourself to feel better. You are allowed to be happy, and no one has the right to take that away.

> *"The key to being happy is knowing you have the power to choose what to accept and what to let go."*[8]
>
> —Dodinsky

So now, whenever I find myself feeling a way I wouldn't like to feel, I apply this technique. I don't apply it to just my feelings. I've applied it to businesses, health, habits, and almost every part of my life.

I call this technique The Three Steps of Change.

**Step 1: Realize**

In order for change to happen, you have to first realize that you need a change. You need to realize you are NOT feeling how you would

---

[8] "The Key to Being Happy Is Knowing You Have the Power to Choose What to Accept and What to Let Go.," Tiny Buddha, February 6, 2017, https://tinybuddha.com/wisdom-quotes/key-happy-knowing-power-choose-accept-let-go/.

like to feel. Knowing you are not where you want to be grants you the understanding to plan your next course of action.

## Step 2: Decide

Then, you need to make a conscious *DECISION* that you will take *ACTION* to go from where you are now to where you wish to be. This step is crucial.

Here's a small example that will explain how and why. Let's say you haven't eaten for the last eight hours, and you realize that you are hungry. However, realizing you are hungry doesn't equate to you going to grab a bite until you decide to take action.

## Step 3: Action

This is where you put things into motion. This is where you take *MASSIVE ACTION*. This is where the rubber meets the road. This is where you will be able to tap into that power within you, where you can take that step towards greatness. You will finally see that you deserve better, you deserve to be loved, and that you can be amazing. This is where you take your decision from Step 2 and put it into the wheels of change.

As in the previous example, this is where you physically stand up, walk into the kitchen, and make a sandwich to eat.

It sounds really simple when associated with hunger and eating or even sleep because it's a need already ingrained in us. However, I believe that our hearts also deserve to feel full and happy. We shouldn't "starve" our hearts of self-love, happiness, and respect, just as we shouldn't starve our physical body of food, water, or rest.

It's not going to be easy, but I'm telling you that it will be absolutely worth it. Following these three steps has allowed me to look at my life in an entirely different way, and today, I am proud to say that I am happy, loved, and filled with gratitude.

I encourage you to apply the three steps of change because I know you deserve better. If you're looking and hoping for someone to change your life today, just know that that person is *YOU*, and you are absolutely worth it.

## BIOGRAPHY

Jameson Chin's career in sales has spanned various companies in Asia for more than a decade, and at his peak, he was selling high ticket items worth six figures. With the knowledge and skills he has acquired, he expanded his field to become a speaker, trainer, and entrepreneur. Sashin Govender, founder and CEO of The Millionaire Student, says, "Jameson has one of the biggest hearts that I know of, and his ultimate goal is to see others succeed. He believes in people more than they believe in themselves." He provides coaching and speaks on sales, entrepreneurship, and motivation. His life goal is to inspire people to take action towards living a life of greatness and not one of mediocrity. Jameson was born and raised in Singapore, and his favorite mantra in times of difficulty is: "When the going gets tough, the tough gets going."

Connect with Jameson Chin via https://linktr.ee/jamesonchin

CHAPTER 17

# How You Want To Be Remembered In Life Is Up To You

*By Javi Utreras*

"Listen, son. The only thing you need to do is create a positive impact on people's lives. When you do this, happiness, money, and success will follow." That is the legacy my dad wanted me to leave for future generations in our family—something that I did not take seriously until I hit the lowest point in my life.

When dealing with people (family, friends, and acquaintances), you have two options: to have them remember you in a positive way; or for them to remember you in a negative way. Which one will you choose, especially if you want to leave a legacy for your family? The choice is yours to make.

At the age of sixteen, I started to work for the second biggest ice cream factory in Ecuador. I started out as a salesperson and, in less than a year, I got promoted to National Sales Supervisor. I handled more than fifteen people in my office. I moved to the US and started working in restaurants. I started out as a dishwasher, and in less than a year, I became General Manager. Later, I got promoted to Manager Partner. I thought I was one of the best in the field because I accomplished company goals, increased profits, and delivered results. But I never got promoted again. I was in shock, and I could not understand until the unexpected (well, expected, based on my decisions) happened. My biggest life lesson hit me one day when my mom was in the shower in my apartment, and the county sheriff came knocking on my door, only to kick me out of my apartment and throw all my stuff on the street. That was one of the most impactful and significant experiences of my life. Sadly enough, I did not learn the lesson until I lost everything again and ended up living in my red Hyundai Excel, taking "showers" in public restrooms, and asking people at the gas station for $5 to fill my car with gas so I could go to work.

This repeated over and over and over: same position, no promotions, no team, no growth in my company, and even worse, no progress in my life. That is when I finally understood what my dad told me for years—something I neither understood nor cared about. Looking back and realizing that I was in the same spot about ten to fifteen years ago, I finally realized that my only focus was on me and what I could get from people (acquaintances, friends, employees, etc.), so I could be the one who shined. I did not care about the people around me, including my family.

My dad was right. So I decided that it was time to make a change in my life. I could not expect different results doing the same thing I did for the past fifteen years. I understood that if I truly wanted to change things around me, I needed to be the first one to change and put a new chip in my head. I had to admit the only way to build something big was to sincerely appreciate people, to teach, coach, and develop them, and be the first to believe in their potential so *they* can achieve their dreams.

I always believe that dealing with people is the most challenging thing in life. We deal with a wide diversity of mindsets, opinions, perspectives, points of view, etc. So, what do we need to do to be successful in dealing with people and creating a positive impact?

When I began to implement some basic concepts to create a positive impact on people's lives, I started a completely different chapter in my life. I started achieving my goals and dreams, but most importantly, the people around me began to do more, and they always saw me as a natural leader who could take them to a different level in their life. I started to develop leaders who developed leaders and created a culture in my team where everyone felt important, appreciated, and enjoyed being part of the journey.

Let me share with you the secret that allowed me to do the following:

1. Grow one of the worst districts in the company, which had only eight stores, to the first one in the region, one of the top five in the company, and with more than seventy stores
2. Dealing with over 250+ employees
3. Build five business with more than 150 employees, with a sales growth of thirty-five percent year after year
4. Develop more than thirty managers, ninety-five percent of whom started out as regular employees
5. Build a team that could run the business for you, generating a residual income while having time for their families
6. Go from living in a red Hyundai Excel to financial freedom

**INVEST IN YOURSELF TO BECOME A BETTER PERSON**

Here is where we, as human beings, struggle the most. We have this old chip in our heads that makes us believe that we will become a better person, a better leader by default, or just by the simple fact our parents were great people that we will inherit the same qualities. Unfortunately, it does not work like that. It is a process that we need to understand and execute ourselves, and we cannot rely on anyone else.

Our minds are like a computer. If you want a computer to do a specific task, you need to program it with a chip, software, program (wherever you want to call it) for the computer to do what you want. Our minds work in the same manner. We need to program them so we start thinking and acting in positive ways, and here is where self-development plays a major role in inspiring others.

You need to become a leader, not a follower. The only way to do that is to invest in yourself by reading about leadership, listening to audiobooks, going to leadership workshops, etc. Why is it so important to start programming your mind to a different mindset? Just for the simple fact that you cannot expect different results doing the same thing over and over; that's what is called insanity. You need to do something different to see different results.

**SHOW SINCERE APPRECIATION FOR PEOPLE**

We have the tendency to reprimand people, yield them when they do something wrong, and show them a nasty attitude, making sure they understand we are "the boss." Well, I have news for you: that does not work at all.

We must show sincere appreciation for people, understand where they are coming from, put ourselves in their shoes, understand their perspectives, listen carefully to their concerns, and never to criticize them (this is the worst thing you can do to someone). Find out what motivates them and what makes them feel important (people love to feel important). Instead of condemning people, try to understand the reasoning behind why they do what they do. If they do something good, laud them for it. Help them to achieve their goals.

When you build a relationship with people based on sincere appreciation, you are developing a relationship that will last forever, and it will create loyalty. People will start following you, and they will jump into the same boat with you to go in the same direction. They will remember you for the rest of their lives as the leader they want to follow and become.

**TEACH, COACH, AND DEVELOP PEOPLE**

A friend of mine who owns a business told me, "You never share everything about the business with your employees because they do not care, and they will try to do something to hurt you." Well, that is the biggest mistake you can make when it comes to building a formidable team. Let's admit it: people love to have the feeling of importance, simple as that. When you spend time with people showing them everything you know, teaching them everything on which you are an expert, develop their leadership skills so they can develop leaders, that is the key to a successful life.

Think about it for a moment. Imagine you have ten people for whom you are responsible, and every single one knows the operation of your business. How often will you struggle if one of them called in sick, did not show to work, or if you had to let them go? How much flexibility will you have when it comes to handling your personal schedule?

Let's be real, the more you teach, coach, and develop people in any area of your life (job, business, family, etc.), the more productive people and freedom you will have.

Now, how often should I do that? Simple, until you die. Teaching, coaching, and developing people is not an overnight or temporary matter. It is an outgoing process that demands consistency. It is not easy, but it will pay off big time.

## STOP THINKING SMALL IS BIG

We all have goals and dreams in life, but dreams without action become wishes. Do not allow people, circumstances, challenges, and distractions to affect the way you dream. Always dream big and never settle for less. The 'why' to your dream needs to be well-established enough that the 'how' becomes abundantly clear. Do not set small goals just because you are scared to say it, to see it, and believe it. I know people will call you crazy or dreamer; they will tell you to be realistic. But the only reality is that you are in control of what you want to achieve in life, and the sky is the limit. When you review your goals and are running short, do not diminish the goal. Instead, increase your activities to achieve them. Write them down twice a day, have them everywhere in your office, house, car, or wherever. Share them with your family and team. See yourself, envision yourself in your goals and dreams every morning so you are the first one to believe.

We were called to be successful in life, so believe in yourself; that is the first step. You set the course for your own destiny; you are the only person who can make it happen. You are capable of doing something big in your life and be successful. You need to understand that success is not something that will happen because of luck. You create your own success just because it is your responsibility, just as it is with your wife, kids, family, company, employer, and society. It is your obligation.

You want to positively impact people's lives, not for your own satisfaction or ego. You want to do it because creating a positive impact in people's life will leave a legacy for all your future generations to remember you as the most powerful and most impactful person in their life.

This is a new beginning in your life where you will face plenty of challenges. Always remember that challenges are meant for you to build your character and become a better person and a better leader.

How you want to be remembered in life is up to you.

## BIOGRAPHY

Javi Utreras is an entrepreneur with more than twenty years of experience building teams, businesses, and developing leaders. His passion for people development and his charisma inspire him to have the vision to create a positive impact on people's lives. His Mission: Helping people achieve big things in their life and generate a residual income that will allow them to become financially independent.

Connect with Javi Utreras via https://linktr.ee/Jutreras

CHAPTER 18

# The Power To Succeed

*By Jessica Okobia*

They say change is the only thing in life that is constant. On November 4th, 1987, I lost my dad. My mum had eight children: four boys and four girls. I am the seventh child. Raising eight children was not that easy for my mum, but she was determined to do so for the sake of her children. She worked as a pharmacist with NNPC (Nigeria National Petroleum Corporation). She is now retired.

I received my Diploma in Petroleum Marketing and Business Studies at the Petroleum Training Institute, Nigeria.

In 2003, I found out that I was pregnant with my first daughter. After my grandmother and my mother-in-law's funeral, I gave birth to her.

My Moving to London

Three years later, my eldest daughter and I moved to London to live with my husband. Coming into England with a diploma from Nigeria, and having no friends, made it challenging for me to find a professional job. So, I had to engage in different training sessions to get into a college.

After a few months of being in England, I was pregnant with my second child. Everything changed; I was sick for three months. My sister-in-law came down to help and took me to get registered at the doctor. The nine months were filled with ups and down: living in a new country, no friends and family. Every day, I prayed to God for strength! My second daughter was born. This time, I was a full-time housewife; I would take my eldest daughter to school and take the little one to a playgroup. Between 2008–2011, I was attending a variety of training sessions. I took various courses such as Microsoft Word, Excel, a class on raising boys, and other courses. Even though I don't have a son, I believe one day I will. I later went to Lewisham College to study Customer Service, where I received a Level II Diploma while pregnant with my third daughter.

My First Degree, BSc Honours

I gave birth to my third daughter. Things were becoming even harder for me during this time, but that did not stop my determination to continue my education. My mother visited from Nigeria for three months to help me with my new-born baby. At this time, I had received a flyer in my letterbox about Plymouth University, and later, my husband saw it on the internet.

I got admission into Plymouth University to study Oil and Gas Management.

Three months later, my mother went back to Nigeria. I had to look for a babysitter to take care of my baby. Things became harder when my mum left because I had to go back to my usual housewife routines while also tackling school assignments, presentations, and readings. During my final year, I got a phone call from my sister in Nigeria informing me of my older brother's death, which was around the time of my final exams. This changed everything. My brother's death shook me and affected me to the point where I couldn't concentrate any longer. The following week was my week of exams.

However, I still dared to write to them. I had my Bible and remembered that I could do all things through Christ who strengthens me (Philippians 4:13). I was still very emotional. I had thought of my brother during one of my exams and started to cry. I later wiped away my tears, thinking about good things, and told myself everything would be alright as I continued my exam. Before my final exams, I decided to apply for my master's at Brunel University in London. I got admission to read project and infrastructure in the Department of Environmental and Civil Engineering.

My Second Degree: Master's in Science

Make My Dream Come Alive

Who says engineering is for men alone? And who says you have to be a genius to study engineering? All you need is INTEREST! Once you desire to become an engineer, don't let anything or anybody discourage you from taking a different path! I love DIY; I don't like waiting for somebody to show me how to fix things.

I got my master's admission only to find out I was pregnant again. The pregnancy was difficult; I was always in and out of the hospital. Finally, I had my baby boy. Two months later, I had to start my master's. My university was an hour and a half away and I travelled three to four times a week to and from there. I was sleep-deprived and had to wait for everyone in my house to fall asleep before I could study to avoid distractions. I would also catch up on reading in the mornings while on the train!

During the year, I was experiencing health problems. But that didn't deter me from studying. I spoke to my supervisor and my course adviser, who advised me to mitigate all the course models. In other words, I had to start my assignments and exams all over again.

These few setbacks did not discourage me from working hard! By this time, my son was about nine months. He struggled to sleep early, which affected me because I wouldn't get enough sleep at night. If it weren't for coffee, I would've slept throughout half my classes. I had success running through the back of my mind! I only held on to positive thoughts, even when it was getting too much for me, and I never thought of quitting. I thought of my future and couldn't look back because I knew that life wouldn't be the same after succeeding.

I recorded my classes on an SD card and downloaded them onto my laptop to re-watch them during my commute. This helped me learn and memorize the content.

At the end of my second term, I got a six-month placement with Environment Agency covering South-East London and Kent. I noticed I was pretty good with my work. That was when I began focusing on environmental studies. I enjoyed working as a flood risk officer, knowing that what I did saved people, animals, and the environment. It changed my mindset on the environment and how we treat it.

When I advise young girls interested in engineering, I ask them to tell me about their interests. I ask them to write down five things they want. Then, they pick their first three and tell me their number one interest. Having a claim and just going with the flow because my friends are doing so is not the best way to pick a profession. Know who you are and why you are doing it. Visualize yourself five years from now. Where will you be? What position will you hold? What training will you have to go through to get to that level?

Ladder of Success

When you want to start your life, you will come across a number of obstacles on the way. A metaphor of life being a ladder will explain what I mean. When you want to start, you start from the bottom step. When you get to the top, and you don't like it, you go down and look for another ladder to climb up. When you climb the next ladder, get to the top, and take in the view from there, you will like what you see.

Be proud of yourself, be ready to start anything. Believe in yourself and never cave-in to negative things or negative people. Let me recount to you what happened to me years ago. Somebody asked me, 'Do you think the BSc you are studying will make me become somebody?' I replied, 'You are not God. I will become what God wills.' That motivated me to go for my master's in Environmental and Civil Engineering. I don't let the gloomy world put me down. Instead, I allow it to motivate me because I am a warrior. I know my children are learning from me.

A friend of mine once saw me reading a book in her house, and she said to me: 'Drop that book. It will blow your brain out,' hinting that there was no way I could read it, possibly calling me dumb. I just laughed at her and never said a word. I just told myself I would study more than her. Negativity like this motivated me rather than pull me down.

I used every negative thing that happened to me to inspire myself, and I did better than I imagined.

That's taking the bull by the horn. How do you maintain thick skin? Don't take criticism hard. Perhaps criticism makes you strong.

Be Grateful

Be grateful for everything you do. It will bring you good tidings from every direction. Do you know what I do every day? I thank God for everything. Looking back at my life, and even now, I am ever grateful. For good times and bad times, I am grateful. The bad times lead me to something good. I have noticed every situation leads you to something. When I have something coming up, I pray for it to come out well. But, if it doesn't, I say: 'God, You know what's best for me even though I may not want it that way.' Later I figure out why God wouldn't grant my request.

WHAT MOTIVATES YOU

Look at the people with whom you spend most of your time. Hold them next to your wealth, health, and happiness. Look at the outcomes these people bring into your life. Are they the right people? Are you on the right part of your life? You spend most of your time with the people with whom you surround yourself. Your outcomes and current situation are most likely the averages of what these people bring into your life. You have to be very intentional with who you choose to surround yourself with.

Start making those shifts in your life today by consciously choosing who and what influences you on a day-to-day basis.

Set your mind on a high level, be creative, be imaginative, be a thinker, be a doer, and take action on things that motivate you. Try new things, stop dwelling on old things. Stop telling yourself, 'I can't do this or that.'

Ask yourself: What do I truly want in life? What is it that brings me joy? Write this down along with your goals. For things to change in your life, you have to change first. Read books, listen to podcasts, attend seminars, network with people, travel, and meet new, like-minded people.

Allow your energy levels to be extremely high; you will end up attracting people with the same energy.

Focus on what you are good at, and you will come out great. Visualize your goals as you begin each day; focus on them and you will never go wrong. I sometimes know that there may be a change of direction.

If you fall on the way, get up, dust yourself, and continue. Falls on the way are a way of setting you back on the right part of life. Learn from every mistake you made in the past so you don't repeat them. You must take challenges if you want to be successful in life. You must examine your mistakes and change who you are.

Expose Yourself to the Right Education

What I do, that every successful person does, is read books, attend seminars, and network with like-minded people. I recommend you do likewise.

Think of something you are passionate about, something you really like doing. Research how you can learn more about it and get involved with organizations that encourage people to invest in what they believe in. Sometimes, we think we don't require anybody's help. On the contrary, everyone needs somebody to help them, whether they like it or not. But know who to trust because there are people out there waiting for you to make a mistake so they can take credit for all your work.

The Power to Scale Through

As a new student, not only do you have a responsibility to yourself to get the most of your studies, you also have group work and group presentations to help inspire and empower others to find their place within the university and its supportive community. That starts by attending lectures.

How to Empower Yourself

The single most effective step you can take during these not-so-ideal times is to surround yourself with people on a similar path and who are willing to share their motivation. This is what creates true empowerment—the empowerment you need to get from where you are right now to where you ultimately want to go.

The Power of the Mind

The mind always plays tricks on you. It will tell you that you can't be like people at the top. Who are the people at the top? Are they better than you, or do they have three heads and four legs? No, of course not. Let your mind always dwell on good things. Think big and grow rich!

We are inspired by what we see every day on the news. Along the way, think of how you can make changes in your life, your community, and your friends. Let them look up to you and say, 'If he or she can make, can I.'

## "NEVER GIVE UP ON YOUR DREAMS UNTIL YOU SUCCEED!"

# BIOGRAPHY

Jessica is an environmental advisor, speaker, coach, and entrepreneur. She inspires humans to consider a relationship with nature, protect the environment, use sustainable development to reduce their carbon footprint, reuse, reduce, and recycle to protect the environment, now and for the future. She loves travelling and networking with others; it is an excellent way to meet new friends with similar hobbies. Her theoretical perspective has earned her opportunities to work on large projects such as Environment Agency, Tideway East, and West Sewage Projects. She designs hats and clothes and encourages young girls in STEM. Jessica has established herself as an entrepreneur. She is married to Charles, with three daughters, Joy, Sophia, Victoria Ethel, and a son, Samuel, in London, UK.

Connect with Jessica Okobia via https://linktr.ee/jessijess

CHAPTER 19

# The Secret Of Your Power

*By Karyne Lauret*

Do you believe in the genie of the lamp?

"Ask, and you will receive. . . ." My mother was a practicing Christian, so I heard this phrase all my childhood.

I was born on a small island, and I grew up in a village where houses were surrounded by sugarcane plantations . . . and nothing else!

My mum was the primary teacher at the village's school, and all the children were afraid of her. She was tough, rigid, and uncompromising, both in school and at home. When I was born, my mum wanted a son. Maybe that was the reason she always behaved as if she reproached me. Feeling rejected by her, I grew up forging myself as a fortress and finding refuge in our garden.

One day, my mother bought a twelve-volume set encyclopedia that was going to affect my childhood. I knew how to read very early on. To escape from my mum's authority, I plunged into a universe of Greek and Roman myths, legends, epics, and fabulous adventures. I created a world around me—a world where monsters, divine creatures, and fantastic heroes were all living together. I believed I was a divinity with special powers, and I was certain to control everything.

Looking for comfort in fairy tales, the genie of the lamp became my best friend, and I asked him everything! In my world, I was convinced I could be, have, and do whatever I wanted to. But as soon as I was back "home," I was a shy, clumsy little girl who was terrified of her mom!

## The World Belongs to Those Who Wake up Early

My mother's parents were impoverished, and she grew up terrorized by an alcoholic and violent father. She didn't want us to be spoiled children, so she would wake us up at 6 am; my brother, sister, and I would have to clean the house, cut the grass, wash the cars—even though we already had a maid and a gardener! We had to execute my mum's orders. Not doing so meant severe punishment.

My mum's mode of education was stringent. Every afternoon, she taught us French history and geography courses. Those were the times that I became secretly rebellious!

When I was eight, my father built a nightclub in our village, and my mother had her fourth child: a boy! In the beginning, it was challenging. We were so far from everything that people would say my father was crazy to think he would succeed!

After six months of going door-to-door to promote the nightclub, the magic happened, and people were coming from everywhere to see what became of the biggest nightclubs on this side of the Indian Ocean.

My parents organized prestigious events. They worked very hard, and their efforts had paid off. While having success, we experienced calamities that would affect my entire life . . . and determine my personality and mindset!

Long story short, my family suffered stabbing attacks, assaults from guns and bladed weapons from different organized gangs, violent battles, death threats, dynamite (overpowered just in time one night), and physical aggression. As the years passed, we'd been burgled many times. One night, my little brother, sister, and I were taken hostage by three armed and hooded men. This ordeal marked us all!

But every time something like this happened, I knew that nothing fatal could happen to us because my genie was protecting us!

When I was ten, my mum brought us to France, and we stayed in a pension for one year. I was happy to be far from home and "independent!"

When we went back home, I weighed ten kilos heavier. My mum became even stricter because we weren't performing well academically.

My mother constantly humiliated me because of my body shape, and I started to lack confidence in myself, living more and more in my bubble. The more I felt rejected and unloved, the worse my bulimia crisis became.

During the summer, my parents used to send us to England for holidays. One day, when going shopping with a new friend, we were arrested by the police because my friend stole some clothes. Even though I was innocent of any crime, my mum refused to believe me. Ever since that day, she considered me as a robber and a liar among the rest. I was eleven years old and totally lost. I was totally distraught by that, and I was angry with my mother for not loving me! I felt more and more rejected and alone!

At the age of twenty, with my university diploma in my pocket, I landed my first job as a teacher. I was elated because I wanted to show my mum that I could earn money all by myself. But I failed miserably when I got inspected a month later. I was completely disoriented. I asked myself: Is this job for me? Do I have to stop? Of course *not*!

*Nothing* in the world would allow me to let my mother rejoice in my failure. Instead, I worked harder. The year after, the inspector came back, and he congratulated me on my evaluation and wished me success in my career. I was so proud of myself because I won.

That year, I got married, and twelve months later, I had my son. My father offered me to come and work with him full time. I was already working with him during the weekends to earn some extra money. He insisted so much that I accepted!

During that time, my parents got divorced. Well, that didn't surprise me because they'd always be quarreling about everything. This was a new beginning for me! I attended a training to learn how to run a business and manage people. We were about thirty employees, primarily men, which made me forge my mindset (because I wanted to be respected by them). No excuses. No complaints. No fear!

One day, we had to face a challenge: my father didn't pay a tax that he contested a few years before. We were asked to pay a large sum of money to be allowed to continue our business. We voluntarily decided to get ourselves under bankruptcy protection. Instead of staying close and committed to restructuring our company and finding the best way to pursue an enhanced future, this caused the beginning of our family's war. On one side were two of my brothers; on the other side, it was my father and me. It was my sister who stayed in the middle and tried to calm everyone down.

The following years were going to be the most challenging times of my life! On January 21, 1999, my sister's office called, informing us that she didn't show up to work, which was unusual. That morning, my brother found my sister hanged herself in her house.

My brilliant sister had put an end to her life. When I arrived at her place, her body was lying on the floor. I begged her to wake up, stroking her bruised neck. I felt like screaming!

'Genie . . . *Why* didn't you protect her? God?!!!'

I had to work the day after, despite my suffering. I don't remember much of my life during this period, except the fact that I couldn't take care of my family (I had two children by that time), and I remained a ghost for a long time, going to the graveyard every night, looking for a sign from my sister. A few months later, I realized that I had to go on living—for me, my father, and my two loving children.

For thirteen years, I kept working with my family, and our relations continued to deteriorate further to a point where it was almost unbearable. We disagreed about everything: the management, the salaries, and the events. We definitely did not have the same vision! In the meantime, I got divorced.

One day, to "protect" my father, I decided to go out and leave twenty years of my life behind me, nothing in my pocket but a strong desire to get out! I didn't know *how*, but I knew *why* I had to accomplish something in my life!

Accepting the Challenge

A year later, the owner of a huge nightclub chain offered me the job of running one of his premier clubs, which he had been unable to start for nearly two years! I hesitated because I didn't want to hurt my father (and even my brothers) by working for this man who was kind of their "enemy." But I was thinking about my strong will to accomplish something great. Above all, I needed to work!

Torn between remorse and the burning desire to accept this job, I said, 'Yes!' No place for tears in this male world. You had to be strong, or you would be eaten. There's no place for the weak!

My rough experiences and education shaped my character, and I was determined to prove to my brothers that I would succeed. It wasn't about directly challenging them, but I had a genuine opportunity to show them (and my mom) that I could start from the bottom and build a prosperous business.

I worked like crazy during the following months! I had no time for me, my life, and my children. I was obsessed with this project, and I had to build a powerful team. I didn't want to be a manager, but a leader, so that I could succeed. We were very united and fueled with passion. Thanks to our perseverance, we became the number one nightclub on the island.

We were organizing amazing events, but we also had to deal with alcoholism, thugs, organized gangs, sometimes working in demanding conditions, and struggling for recognition from our boss.

Those years were some of the greatest moments of my life, and I built solid and eternal friendships with people from my team. We had succeeded. But deep inside, I wanted something else.

A New Milestone

One night, while working, I received a call. My father had fallen off a ladder and was placed in intensive care with a severe brain hematoma. This gave me flashbacks of my sister. But at that moment, I refused to think of anything negative! Even though he looked better the day after, my father fell into a coma in the middle of the night. The doctor announced to us that my father wouldn't live!

The days that followed were horrifying. I didn't leave him, praying to God, my dear genie, and all the powers of the Universe for his healing and a miracle! Five days into his coma, my dad passed away before my eyes. It felt like my heart was ripped out! I had been powerless to save him and keep him in my life. Since I was a child, I viewed my father as an everlasting figure. My whole world was falling apart. I didn't go to work in the following weeks. I stayed at home, crying, refusing to eat, cut from the world . . . shredded!

One night, on the insistence of a friend who introduced me to a travel concept just before my dad's accident, I agreed to go on a trip with her. A little voice was telling me to accept and that this decision was to mark a turning point in my life!

For the past two years, I've been all around the globe, meeting fantastic people and experiencing many new things. I'm stronger than ever. The only things that count are my family, passions, goals, freedom, being happy, and making people happy!

I have time for my children, and for the first time ever, my mum told me, 'I love you!' I thank her for who I am today.

Life challenges us, but we must keep going as long as we have a great vision, belief, and passion in our hearts! More than ever before, I know that I am here for a purpose. I've realized that my genie has always been me! Now that I have become aware of my power, I wish to help as many people as possible!

The Universe has given me what I deserve! I have stopped fighting, and I know the next thirty years will be different! The best is yet to come!

# BIOGRAPHY

Karyne Lauret has worked for the longer part of her existence as a manager in big nightclubs. Having provided support to individuals impacted by daily stress, struggles, and the chaos of modern life, she has developed a strong sense of helping people, with a passion for human beings in general. She has raised her voice for justice, equity, and compassion for herself and others all her life. Today, she is an entrepreneur and works in a world where personal development is a full part of her living, making others' fulfillment and freedom a priority.

Connect with Karyne Lauret via https://linktr.ee/Karyn_Lauret

CHAPTER 20

# StEPs: They All Count!

*By Kaydell Barron*

How many steps do you take in a day? The American Heart Association recommends a person take 10,000 steps a day. That is about five miles (8,046.72 meters) of movement.[9] Do you really need 10,000 steps? Maybe. Maybe not.

A bit of trivia. Further research regarding the whole 10,000-steps-a-day concept uncovers that the number wasn't necessarily based on health science at all. Rather, it was first suggested as part of a marketing campaign for a Japanese manufacturer of pedometers.[10]

Research has shown that mortality rates decrease with an increase in the number of steps you take, but the benefits level off at approximately 7,500 steps.[11] Just increasing daily physical activity by as little as 2,000

---

9  Steve Chen and Kathleen Coxwell, "The American Heart Association Recommends 10,000 Steps a Day or About Five Miles of Walking," NewRetirement, June 17, 2020, https://www.newretirement.com/retirement/the-american-heart-association-recommends-10000-steps-a-day-or-about-five-miles-of-walking/.

10  Claire Maldarelli, "This Epidemiologist Proved 10,000 Steps Is a Lie," Popular Science, April 26, 2021, https://www.popsci.com/story/health/10000-steps-evidence-study/.

11  Steve Calechman, "10,000 Steps a Day - or Fewer?" Harvard Health, July 11, 2019, https://www.health.harvard.edu/blog/10000-steps-a-day-or-fewer-2019071117305.

steps (less than a mile of walking) can have positive health outcomes.[12] We can all take 2,000 steps a day—most of us do that without even realizing it.

However, stop moving, and our bodies react immediately. Researchers studied a group of healthy adults as they decreased their daily activity. The volunteers cut the number of steps they took each day by at least half. This more sedentary lifestyle had an immediate, negative impact on the health markers of each participant. Within the first day of inactivity, the volunteers' blood sugar levels spiked significantly after meals, and the levels climbed with each subsequent day of inactivity.

Why do I bring this up? Why is it significant to a person's success?

Taking steps and taking them daily—any number of steps, any type of steps—will move you closer to your success. Standing still hinders progress. I have realized that each step taken is progress. So whether you choose (or are able to take) 10,000 steps, or just ten, or maybe step in place on any given day, they all count!

Big steps. Little steps. Quick steps. Slow steps. Steps forward. Steps backward. Steps together. Steps apart. Easy steps. Hard steps. Steps with purpose. Steps with no intended direction. Steps uphill. Steps downhill. Steps to the side. And lastly, steps in place. There are no wrong steps. All steps help you reach your success.

Grasping this concept is important because we tend to discount steps taken that may not be obvious and directly measurable to our stated goal and personal definition of success. I invite you to realize that every one of us benefits from all the steps we have taken and will continue to take on our unique journeys.

*"A journey of a thousand miles begins with a single step" is a common saying that originated from a famous Chinese proverb. The quotation is from Chapter 64 of the Dao De Jing ascribed to Laozi.[13] This saying teaches that even the*

---

12  Ibid.
13  Derek Lin, "Tao Te Ching – Chapter 64," Taoismnet, accessed June 2, 2021, https://taoism.net/tao/tao-te-ching-chapter-64/.

longest and most difficult ventures have a starting point, which begins with one first step.

Another way to remind yourself that daily momentum will bring you closer to your success is to use StEP as an acronym for "Success through Everyday Progress." Achievements **are made through small but concrete actions.** Dreams and life goals are achieved by making a plan and taking the first step towards them.

A child's first step is an eventful milestone (maybe even considered a Kodak moment for those of us that know what "Kodak moments" are). That first step carries so much significance. It begins a child's unique path to wherever he/she decides to venture in this life and marks the beginning of their independence. And yet, who remembers taking that first step? My guess would be almost none of us. I say this because even though we may not actually remember our first step, we all know its importance. All of our steps have importance; they got us to where we are now. From the knowledge and wisdom gained from those historical steps, we can evaluate the direction we wish to take our next step.

At eighteen, I was so sure of my life's journey—what my definition of success was, my S.M.A.R.T. goals, and the age I was going to achieve all of them.

A quick side note. S.M.A.R.T. is a mnemonic acronym providing criteria to assist in setting goals and objectives on a person's journey to success. To help a person determine if an objective has been met, the goal should be **S**pecific, **M**easurable, **A**ttainable, **R**elevant, and **T**ime-based.[14]

I had the confidence that I could and would overcome any obstacle in my way. I knew where I was going to live and with whom I was going to share my life and my journey. I had a very structured plan and measured it out. I am a numbers person—an accountant by degree. I was set, full

---

14 "SMART Goal - Definition, Guide, and Importance of Goal Setting," Corporate Finance Institute, September 16, 2020, https://corporatefinanceinstitute.com/resources/knowledge/other/smart-goal/.

speed ahead: earn my degree; advance in Corporate America; marry and have a family; big steps; quick steps; steps forward; and steps together.

Stand Still. I am sure you know that life presented me with more than one detour away from this original, well-defined plan. And I don't need to bother telling you how different my steps became. I did earn my degree in accounting (Big Step Forward). I never really had a passion for the work. It was a job—just a way to earn money to afford the other "pleasures" in life (Step in Place)—but not a good way to step through each and every workday. I married my high school sweetheart (Step Together). Unfortunately, our union did not survive the test of time (Step Apart). I loved him so very much. I am so grateful for the untarnished love we had. I have no regrets about those shared steps.

Life goes on whether you want it to or not. I kept stepping.

At thirty-three, I realized most of the steps I took were those with no intended direction, and most of them felt like I was only stepping uphill. It was time to stop aimlessly wandering in the desert of my life. Yet, I realized that these steps over this time period were not wasted steps. I invite you also to realize that any and all steps you have already taken are not wasted. You have learned something. You have experienced something. Take advantage of that knowledge. I did. I began stepping again with purpose. I relocated to Atlanta, Georgia, to start a redirected career path. With this move, I also had the unexpected experience of being able to step with newness in myself. I was on my own; I only knew one person in Atlanta when I moved there. I was taking big steps forward while leveraging the steps I had already taken. My definition of success had not really changed from when I was eighteen, but how I measured success and the goals I set were different. I was experiencing the joy of my journey.

At forty-seven, life presented my family with an unexpected detour. My father was diagnosed with brain cancer. The day after his diagnosis, without hesitation, I resigned from my position as Vice President of Business Development of a consulting firm to help my mother care for him. I was a Daddy's girl, so it was an easy choice to take care of him. His quality of life remained good for the next ten months. His eleventh month was spent in hospice care. All my steps had a new purpose and a different energy behind them. I was definitely on a different path than I had ever been. After my father's death, my focus shifted to the care of my mother. She had never truly lived alone. She and my father had been married for fifty-seven years. I am still my mother's primary caregiver today. In these past thirteen years, we have experienced typical mother-daughter conflicts. We both experience frustration and fear as aging affects us. However, I know I would make the same decision of changing my journey's course again to take care of my parents. Doing so has been a privilege. This detour permanently changed the trajectory of my life.

At sixty, my journey brings me here. We have all participated in a crazy couple of years leading up to today. Many of our journeys have been impacted by external forces that we did not anticipate. For historical reference and perspective, I am referring to the COVID-19 global pandemic and the political tension and social unrest experienced in the United States. These events and their related consequences have altered each of our journeys forever. We each may have to rethink our plans, restructure our finances, and re-map our projected paths. We are in a state of new "normal." And we all are trying to navigate successfully. I would like to remind each of us that we can succeed through everyday progress by taking just one step—even if it is in place—to keep the momentum going to obtain our own personal success. Today, I am counting words rather than steps. This chapter is to be 2,000 meaningful words that express my philosophy of success and how to experience it daily. I am counting them because they are helping me realize a new level of personal success and growth. They are my new steps.

I remind myself to breathe with each word just as if I were running a marathon (I have not actually run a marathon before, but I have rowed a half-marathon). I am out of my comfort zone. I am out of my protective bubble. Until I decided to participate in this book project, I wanted to be "anonymous." I wanted to be successful, but I didn't want to have attention called to me. I blush pretty easily. I wanted to share my experience, but I wanted to do it virtually through an avatar. Now I have some new, crazy, big dreams and goals. And I am planning to take daily steps to ensure progress toward making these dreams a reality.

My life's mission can be paraphrased as "I want to make sure the lives that are touched by mine are made better for it," If you are reading this, then I am touching your life. How can I make it better? Hopefully, you have a new appreciation of yourself and your journey up to this point. All the previous steps you have taken have brought you here. They have provided you with the experience, knowledge, and wisdom of what you want, don't want, need, don't need, and aspire to accomplish.

Your previous path has shown you which direction to venture next to give you the faith and hope for a successful tomorrow. I encourage you to StEP. Big steps. Little steps. Quick steps. Slow steps. Steps forward. Steps backward. Steps together. Steps apart. Easy steps. Hard steps. Steps with purpose. Steps with no intended direction. Steps uphill. Steps downhill. Steps to the side. And lastly, steps in place. There are no wrong steps. All steps help you reach your success.

Now I want to add *Dance Steps*. I want to celebrate each of us. I want to celebrate our dreams. I want to celebrate our progress. I want to share steps on our unique journeys.

I intend to be stepping in Success through Everyday Progress (StEP). I encourage you to make that same intention.

## BIOGRAPHY

Kaydell Barron is a native Texan who is currently a full-time caregiver, entrepreneur, student of life, and author of *StEPs: They All Count!* Seeking personal success and celebration of life in the everyday, Kaydell reminds us all to learn from our pasts, to have hope and faith for our futures, and to live in the gift of the present. Kaydell is a member of Success Publishing and Authors Group. Step into your success. Dance into your celebration.

Connect with Kaydell Barron via https://linktr.ee/kaydell_barron

CHAPTER 21

# Fat, Ugly, Queer To Fabulous And Successful Business Professional Mindset: Overcoming Everyday Obstacles, Negativity, And Self-Doubt To Create A Perfect New You!

*By Larry C. LeSueur*

Although I am forty-six years old now. I still have the forever memories of my childhood drilled and embedded into my brain, heart, and soul! I can remember being called "fat, queer, and f****t, among other things, more times than I can count. I vividly recall my anger, shame, embarrassment, agony, anguish, torture, self-hatred, and utter loathing of grade school and high school. I remember continuously combatting and denying the accusations of homosexuality, but I suppose it's near impossible to convincingly convey my heterosexuality when indeed it was and is a lie. Equally, I reminisce growing up in a Baptist Church where I was regularly indoctrinated that I was an abomination in the eyes of God and that my ultimate destiny was an endless life of BURNING IN HELL! My number one mission back then was to keep my sexuality from my family at all costs, especially my biological father, whose everyday vocabulary incorporated 'queer' and 'f*****' My parents divorced shortly after my turning sixteen. I reluctantly chose to live with my biological father and his new, almost immediate wife so that I would not have to change schools.

My drug and alcohol problem intensified with the divorce. I found myself taking a thermos of vodka to school every day (on days I actually made it) to make it through. I would continue further with pot, cocaine, crystal meth, and anything else that I thought would take away my never-ending thoughts, pain, and fears. I feared my family hating me. I had no friends who knew the true me (I did have one great friend in school, Chris, but he never knew about my sexuality, and I eventually ghosted him, fearing he would find out and end our friendship). There was no one to talk to, and I felt all alone. I remember becoming suicidal; I remember hoarding pills for that purpose. I remember holding the loaded .38 caliber revolver, kept on the top of the dresser topper of my parents' bedroom, to my head countless times without the courage to pull the trigger. I remember crying out, 'I cannot even kill myself! What a true piece of shit I am!' Besides my amazing mother and grandmother, Carolyn and Margaret, I cannot recall one positive image of myself during those years. I recollect the feelings of utter hopelessness and complete despair, feeling nothing would ever change. I remember my mother sitting/laying with me on countless nights, sharing in my tears, consoling me, and letting me know it would all be okay. She never knew the true depth of my anguish and torment because I wouldn't dare let her know I was a f** atop of all my other problems. Turning sixteen and attaining a driver's license would further intensify the drug and alcohol problem. Not to mention opening a whole new door to promiscuous sex with random men to fuel my need for attention (to feel loved and accepted for who I was) and desire to escape reality. The reality was that I was living a life of lies, hiding and pretending to be someone else to conform to what I thought my family, my God, and society wanted. My promiscuous lifestyle (I hate that word, homosexuality is **NOT** a lifestyle), drugs, and alcohol eventually made me drop out of high school just two weeks before graduation. Now, on top of being a fat, ugly, useless f*****, I was a high school dropout as well (I did sign up to get my GED almost immediately upon quitting high school; one positive).

Then came the inevitable day I kidded myself would never happen. My mother discovered my deepest, most hidden secret: I'm gay. This is a very long story, and for time's sake, we will skip this. To say my life turned upside down would be a huge understatement. I still recall sitting at her white kitchen table and her telling me I had to tell my father and that if I did not, she would, because he deserved to know the truth. Feeling that it would be better coming from me than her, I decided to tell him myself. I still vividly recount that awkward conversation. I made sure my uncle was there as I feared and expected the worst possible outcome. I fully expected him to kill me, or at the very least, beat the ever-living hell out of me! I still picture today the look of anger, rage, dismay, disappointment, detest, and hatred in his eyes and face as he glared at me in what felt like an eternity of silence. I don't recall the exact sequence of events that immediately followed the revelation. However, the outcome was that he changed the locks to the house, told me I had two days to get "my shit" out of his house, or he would put it in the front yard and burn it. I recall renting a U-Haul as a minor (no easy feat) and wondering how I would get all my furniture and stuff in it once I got it there. I lovingly remember my grandmother, Margaret, telling me to move into her basement. Thus, I moved into my grandmother's basement, and unlike so many other gay youths, I was not homeless. Thank you, Granny! Throughout this entire family coming-out process, Granny was the only person who never treated me any differently, never changed the way she looked at me, never changed the way she talked to me, never changed anything about just being my Granny! She has passed away since then, and I miss her every day. But I am sure she knows what a true blessing and lifesaver she was to me! Needed note: this coming out was near the AIDS crisis in America, and I'm sure that influenced my mother's actions and decisions. My mother had always been my rock, my one true friend, and now, my mother told me that she still loved me and that would never change. However, lots of subtle things did change: she would rarely look me in the eye when talking to me; she would not eat or drink after me; and our once open and robust conversations were now merely hellos, goodbyes, and small talk. I think of her echoing my childhood pastor saying I would burn in Hell for all Eternity! There's another long, in-depth story about how my mother's views and relationship with me evolved, but again, for the sake of time, we will skip that. Let's just say that my mother, Carolyn, is once again my best friend, my rock, my number one fan, my everything. I cannot imagine a life without her love, care, empathy, compassion, and overall greatness! Thank you, Mom, for everything you've done for me, taught me, given me, and continue to do. I love you with all my heart!

Then comes Carla (one of my worst decisions and regrets). Long story short, Carla and I went to high school together. Neither were we friends nor did we even associate with each other in high school. Carla got hired at a Hardee's I was working, and as a joke, we pretended to be married (after taking a coincidental vacation at the same time). I did this to get someone at Hardee's to leave me alone, someone who had been harassing me for some time then. This was a guy, and I was still in the closet, and he would jeopardize everything if he outed me. Carla and I went on a couple of dates, and voila, it worked. The guy completely quit talking to me. My mind began racing with thoughts of how this could have helped with so many other family problems. With little thought or preparation, I proposed to Carla two weeks later, and we were married. I was right; this did repair my relationship with my biological father. Although my mother did not like Carla, she seemed to be happy with the idea. Granny, on the other hand, was not so thrilled. But it did happen, and for the next year, I remained a faithful and committed husband to Carla. I was by no means or stretch of the imagination a heterosexual, and sex was an incredibly challenging matter, to say the least. How she did not figure it out, given some of the most awkward sexual encounters in history, is still a mystery to me. I remember calling out to God daily in prayer, sometimes multiple times a day: "God, if I am supposed to be straight and with a woman, let me fall in love with Carla. Fulfill our marriage with a child, show me the way to make this work and . . ." It was as if my prayers were falling on deaf ears, and nothing changed. My desire to be with a man was driving me crazy.

A year into my faithful marriage, giving it every opportunity, I knew what I had to do. I went to Carla and confessed I was gay and wanted a divorce. It's a very long and messy story, but the marriage drug out for another year and a half before the divorce was finalized. I even filed bankruptcy as an eighteen-year-old during this process. To this day, I feel horrible about marrying Carla. I am sure this was brutal for her, and I have no way of knowing how this ultimately affected her. With that being said, many reasons went into my decision to marry her. The primary reason being trying to reconcile my religious beliefs and forego the eternal 'Hell and Brimstone' I had shoved down my throat all the time. Since this time, my religious views have evolved. I do consider myself, and happily pronounce to the world, a gay, proud Christian who owes his life and success to Christ Jesus, my masterful Creator, who does not make mistakes. I will discuss how Jesus saved my life more than once in the coming paragraph.

If I were to point to one particular event that ultimately prevented me from killing myself, it would be becoming a truck driver. You read that right—an eighteen-wheel truck driver. My original intent with going to Alliance Truck Driving School was to escape my wife, Carla. Little did I know, it would open my eyes to another world. Becoming a truck driver was not easy, and there was a huge learning curve for this queer from Northeast Tennessee. Eventually, I became beyond proficient and spent the next nine years being a driver trainer for new OTR (over the road) drivers. Driving a truck took me all over the United States. It showed me that there were so many other places that were nothing like Northeast Tennessee. It showed me a great number of major cities where people simply did not give a shit about who I loved, my preferences, or anything else for that matter. A couple of divine interventions took place while driving as well.

1. While I was on I-81N, leaving Virginia and entering West Virginia, traveling sixty-eight miles per hour, the wet roads suddenly became a solid sheet of ice. I recall the truck and trailer

going sideways up the interstate at sixty-eight miles per hour. I was heading for a concrete pylon holding up an overhead bridge. I could hear the steer tires digging into the gravel of the median as I flew toward my inevitable death. I locked my elbows on the wheel, braced myself, and closed my eyes, waiting for impact. After what seemed like five minutes but was probably five seconds, I opened my eyes only to be heading completely straight down the interstate with no foreseen danger at all.

2. Everyone who has driven the interstate system throughout the US knows how rare left-hand exits are. While traveling north on I-95 in Connecticut, I was going approximately sixty-eight miles per hour, and apparently, I fell asleep at the wheel. I suddenly woke up and was mere seconds from rear-ending a stopped tractor trailer in traffic. It just so happened that there was a left-hand exit right there at that moment. It was a sharp curve and was meant to be taken at a very low speed, probably thirty or less, but I whipped the wheel to the left and went through the curve at God-only-knows-what speed while stomping the brake, which should have made the situation even worse. Through divine intervention, the truck remained upright, unscratched, and no one was harmed or killed. I did have to stop, change clothes, and regroup from this near-death experience.

I bring up both of these events as I will never forget to thank God for sparing me. Both times, I remember praying: "If I am a queer and an abomination in your eyes, then why would you spare me? Why not let me die and be done?" While I never got a verbal answer, I believe it is because I have something to offer this world, and someone down the line may need me. I believe that my sexuality and who I love are not sins, and God couldn't care less that I love someone even if he is a man. Love is Love, and Love always wins over Hate! God is Love!

After driving a truck, I opened a retail store and closed it in 2008 with the economic collapse. During this time in the store, I discovered the movie *The Secret* from one of my best customers, Diane, which explains the importance of mindset, emotions, and the laws of attraction. I'm eternally grateful to her for this discovery; it changed and explained so much. I have since read and listened to so many other related books and audiobooks that have equally enriched my life beyond words. I learned that I can be whatever I want as long as I want it bad enough, envision it, and work for it. Negativity brings more negativity. But thankfully, positivity brings more positivity.

While I have experienced more setbacks and obstacles (way more than I can cover in this book) to overcome, my newfound mindset, positivity, faith, and zeal for life have afforded me an amazing and rewarding life. These days, I love helping others in many different ways. I work as a registered nurse in an emergency department where I get to help others and sometimes even save lives. I am a Pride Coordinator with the local union where I work. I am the LGBT Special Emphasis Program Manager at the hospital and the Chair of the EEO/Diversity Committee. I have and continue to proudly work with local Pride organizations in the area. I am a marketing executive for a few different direct sales companies that help people in so many ways. I own a marketing company that specializes in marketing consulting, retail packaging, screen printing/embroidery/applique/laser/sublimation/heat printing of apparel, printing an array of marketing materials, forms, checks, and so forth, creating signs/banners/table covers/tradeshow displays, promotional products, performing direct mail campaigns, managing social media accounts, graphic design, incentive programs, service awards, corporate gifts, and more. This allows me to help other business owners become successful and devise plans to solve problems and attain goals. I am a real estate professional where I get the honor of helping others in their quest for residential and commercial properties. I am currently exploring a new business opportunity in the health and wellness arena with a focus on weight management; I'm sure you will hear of this in the future as it comes to fruition. I don't share all this to brag or boast but to illustrate that no matter what life throws your way, with the proper mindset, motivation, work, and dedication, you can do anything, be anyone, and be your version of FABULOUS! I will end this chapter with two of my all-time favorite quotes, both of which happen to come from Zig Ziglar: "You will get all you want in life if you help enough people to get what they want." and "If you can dream it, you can achieve it."[15] My ultimate goal behind this chapter and book is to let you know that you can do what you want and be who you want to be, no matter where you come from, what your situation is, what you have, or what you don't have. I sincerely hope that this story has helped someone, and if so, my mission is complete with this work. Thank you so much for taking the time to read this. May you have a blessed, rich, and Fabulous life!

## BIOGRAPHY

Larry C. LeSueur, BSN, RN, Author, Business Owner, and Speaker, is a lifelong resident of the Johnson City, TN area but has traveled extensively throughout the United States, enriching his culture and diversity. In addition to his BSN degree, he has done extensive continuing education in Marketing/Advertising, Health, Healthcare, Wellness, and Real Estate. This education has cemented his success as a Registered Nurse, Health & Wellness Coach, and Real Estate Professional. Mr. LeSueur was very vulnerable and honest with this book, showcasing one of his deepest secrets that caused him much shame and ridicule, and more as a young adult. Sadly, even today, this has the potential to cause him great harm from a business perspective. His bravery amplifies his belief that truth,

---

15   Kevin Kruse, "Zig Ziglar: 10 Quotes That Can Change Your Life," Forbes (Forbes Magazine, July 8, 2013), https://www.forbes.com/sites/kevinkruse/2012/11/28/zig-ziglar-10-quotes-that-can-change-your-life/?sh=23a0a9d526a0.

honesty, and integrity win every time over fake personas. This must-read demonstrates overcoming some of the hardest things one can imagine is possible and that with the right mindset, vision, and determination, anything one wants in life is attainable.

Connect with Larry C. LeSueur via https://linktr.ee/LarryLeSueur

CHAPTER 22

# The Secret Of Resurrecting Your Purpose Of Life Through Creating A "Dream-Board"

*By Lena Jo*

It's during times like these when I feel I am fully living my purpose. This is my passion: to love people and drive them into a new way of thinking about themselves and to help them find *their* purpose, to guide them in daring to imagine extraordinary dreams for the future. When I see *their* dreams come to life in *their* minds and witness their faces illuminate with a new glow, I know I am living my purpose. That is worth EVERYTHING.

I knew, from an early age, that I was called to add value to people's lives. But sometimes, becoming that person does not go as planned. Surely, it was not part of *my* "dream board." All I saw was the highway to success with a line of happy people on the sidelines cheering me on because I inspired them to a life of fulfilment.

If I only had foreseen what I wished for!

Little did I know that to inspire others, I had to first go through hell. To become a diamond that cuts through others' pain, I had to first be that little piece of black coal placed under tremendous pressure—more pressure than I thought I could endure. Then I could mirror their hidden greatness and make them see themselves in that reflection.

I am Lena, from Sweden. I'm a wife to a loving husband and a mother of three. I am a physiotherapist, family counsellor, pastor, teacher, business owner, network marketing distributor, a John Maxwell and Mars Venus gender intelligence life and business coach, author, and artist. But the most important title I hold is 'Child of God,' a daughter to the King, and that is what makes all the difference. If I didn't have God in my life, I do not know how I would have endured all my toughest experiences. When you have the benefit of living up to a mature age, life will hit you sooner or later.

I was brought up in a safe and loving Christian environment. Given that, I couldn't believe that anyone would opt me out of their life—not when they had once chosen to love me and decided to build a future with me. But that was exactly what happened. After being married for just one and a half years, I was left alone and devastated, without getting an answer as to why, with all my dreams scattered—and I was only twenty-four. My future, as I had imagined it, was gone. Would I ever have a family of my own? What was my purpose? I was beaten and knocked down *but not counted down*.

The Bible tells us that we will not have to endure trials beyond our capability (1 Corinthians 10:13 NUB). When I read that, I thought: 'Oh, so *this* is how strong I am? Really?' I also remembered that it says in Jeremiah, in the same great book, that God saw me in his thoughts already before I was conceived in my mother's womb (Jeremiah 1:5). I was part of His "dream-board" before I was born. WOW! There was a purpose in my life, even if I couldn't see it right then and there. God wanted me to be here for a time like this. I was a part of His plan for this age . . . *and so are you.*

What a magnificent thought.

It was there that I decided that I wouldn't succumb to bitterness. I knew that bitterness only punished the bitter person, not the one with whom you are bitter, and that bitterness rots the bones. I desired to live my life to the fullest, no matter how people treated me. I forgave, and I told God that if the person I loved didn't want to love me or be loved by me, I would dedicate my life to love people who *wanted* my love, who *needed* my love, and who *let* me love them.

When I had graduated as a physiotherapist, I began working at a rehabilitation centre for young people with neurological disabilities. I started to love these precious people with everything I had. I found a purpose in life. And I found that God has a purpose for everyone. *No one else* can decide if a person has a purpose or not. Just the fact that you are here on this earth indicates you have a purpose. It doesn't matter if your parents thought it was a mistake that you were conceived. It doesn't matter if the condom broke and that's why you are here today. It doesn't even matter if you are the result of a rape or abuse. *You are not a mistake. You* are planned by the King of Kings and the Lord of Lords, regardless of what leads up to you being here. *You* were on *His* "dream-board" long before that ever happened. *You* are here because you have a purpose, because you are you, and no one else can replace you.

Let no one ever tell you that you have no purpose being here. Who has the right to decide that, when God, the Creator Himself, has given you life and put you here for a purpose?

I especially remember a young girl from the rehabilitation centre. She was in her mid-twenties and was disabled. She had deformed legs and feet, had to get around with a wheelchair, and had no sensibility. Due to this, she experienced several accidents and burned herself, which had resulted in amputated fingers. She had to look in the mirror when eating to be able to place the spoon into her mouth because she had no sense of touch.

Perhaps you think that she would not be able to find her purpose in life. I asked her if she rather wouldn't have been born. She looked at me in shock. She replied: 'Of course not! I love life!'

In spite of all her troubles and plagues, she had a joyous sense of life that I have not seen in many people. She fully lived out her life and added value to all around her. The last time I contacted her, she was married and worked as a priest in a church, being a shepherd to her flock. She really had found her purpose in life, and many have had the privilege of being helped by her. She said YES to being a part of God's plan for her life. She could have had a thousand reasons to say NO, but she didn't. She said YES!

Have you found your purpose in life? Big or small? Have you said YES to your purpose in life? Are you grateful that you, once upon a time, were a part of God's "dream-board?" Or are you a victim of circumstances?

I am not a hero in this world, but I do know that even if it was just because I was to show love to people around me, I would be living my purpose. The greatest purpose has been to see my kids grow up and come to realize *their* purpose in life.

Constantly trying to increase my ability to inspire change in people's life also expanded my own horizons. Although I cannot help everyone, I want to ignite a spark inside everyone I meet. I want them to know that they can do something with their lives, something they never thought possible. I want them to find *their* purpose.

Of course, it is marvellous speaking to a big audience where everyone is familiar with the

concept of dreaming big. To help others visualize, to pave the way for a future with thoughts built on faith, and faith being the hope for things we do not yet see.

I do have a vision of speaking to big crowds, filling up fields as far as my eyes can see, but my highest passion is to be the tool that builds faith in people that have *no* faith, who have never experienced the luxury of dreaming big. These wonderful people's everyday struggle is to survive, find food, and shelter. Their lives are left with no strength to create the path to what God's purpose may be in their life. They are left to just let life pass, one day at a time.

When I was a teenager, I wanted to let Jesus be Lord of my life, but I was nervous that he would send me to Africa as a missionary; and I did not want to go to Africa. But after a while, I thought that if He *really* wanted to send me to Africa, I suppose I surely would have an urge to go there. But I didn't, so I decided it would be risk-free to take the leap and live my life as a dedicated Christian. I find it amusing that wherever I go,

I always end up meeting African people who become my best friends or like second family. It is as if my heart has the same

heartbeat as Africa. God has a sense of humour, doesn't He?

In 2015, many migrated to Sweden for refuge, from war, personal or political abuse, or from

poverty. Many sold all their possessions to be able to cross the globe and come to Sweden. Some lost loved ones on the escape over the Mediterranean Sea. One of my friends had been swimming for eight hours in the dark night after the escape boat caught fire, all the while hearing screams of help from the people in the water. With each passing hour, the screams got quieter and quieter. When you survive such a trauma, you only want to come into safety. All other dreams are hidden deep inside of you or thrown away.

Even in my little town in the countryside, we received hundreds of refugees from Syria,

Afghanistan, and other countries, but mostly from Eritrea. In the end, I didn't have to go to

Africa to find my purpose. Africa came to me.

I started a Swedish class in church, which I held every week for two years. After that, the community asked if I could come and teach Swedish to the refugees at their school.

My main purpose with the lessons was not to teach Swedish (even if that was what I did) but to fill the students with faith, dreams, and visions for the future. So many of my students were not able to dream. What a joy to see them fully occupied putting a "dream-board" together and proudly present it to the class. A year later, I witnessed some of their dreams coming true.

Helping my students connect and become friends with people from countries other than their own was a tremendous joy to me. To break isolation and dare to be themselves was the purpose of my communication class. Many didn't want to connect with each other. They were afraid of making fools of themselves in front of each other. Because of this, few wanted to speak in front of the class. So, I created a lot of crazy teambuilding exercises. At the beginning of the year, they were rather angry at me for putting them through all the exercises. But the whole class had ultimately transformed. They were connecting in new ways, meeting during weekends, and interconnecting as a family. They stretched themselves and presented fantastic speeches for the graduation.

It's during times like these when I feel I am fully living my purpose. This is my passion: to love people and drive them into a new way of thinking about themselves and to help them find *their* purpose, to guide them in daring to imagine extraordinary dreams for the future. When I see *their* dreams come to life in *their* minds and witness their faces illuminate with a new glow, I know I am living my purpose.

That is worth EVERYTHING.

Every person is here for a purpose. So are you!

## BIOGRAPHY

Lena Jo is a coach who awakens dreams and helps clients find their purpose in life. *Women with purpose: Achieve the life of your dreams, without sacrificing your values or dignity* is her upcoming book on personal growth. Sweden's most successful female network marketing leader's life stories, together with her teachings on how to achieve a life with purpose, are a must. Lena is an appreciated speaker, co-author of devotional books, and founder of the women's event "Daughter to the King." She is a constant learner, physiotherapist, family counselor, pastor, teacher, business owner, direct selling distributor for Zinzino, a certified John Maxwell coach and speaker, a Mars Venus gender intelligence life and business coach, author, and an artist with life-affirming paintings. The most important thing in her life is her family. She has been happily married to Sven for thirty years and is a really proud mum to Josef, Sofie, and Lukas.

Connect with Lena Jo via https://linktr.ee/Lenajo

CHAPTER 23

# A Tale Of Love, Setbacks, And Successes

*By Michael Wesley*

I've always been a problem-solver, and I've learned to be a survivor. I never quit!

I've always been striving towards something better. But I am about to tell you how I sunk to the lowest point of my life and how I got out of it.

Feeling unloved and unconnected to the people in my surroundings, being bullied during all my school years for being different, I often thought about taking my life. I felt worthless!

I knew my parents loved me, but no one else seemed to—including me. Therefore, I was shocked to one day experience myself at my wedding, marrying a woman who loved me as much as I loved her.

I had always been afraid of being on stage; I hated people having their focus on me. But this time, I couldn't hide. My scout leader friends from church, where I had been a leader for many years, had prepared plenty of fun and games for that day. So, the only alternative I had was to release my fears and play along. It was fun and deliberating. That was the start of my personal development journey.

A few years later, having a three-year-old daughter and one-year-old twins, my wife wanted a divorce. I was devastated, and I didn't understand why. Being in shock, I did not have the capacity to listen to everything she said.

But from what I picked up, she was right! It took me just a few hours to realize that she was right, and that I was about to lose the best things in my life. In a feeling of calm panic, I had two questions:

*Do you still love me?*
*Are you willing to work on making this a loving marriage?*

She said **Yes** to both questions. A **No** to either question would have ended the marriage. From this experience, I learned to shift my focus from myself to others, become humbler, and use my two ears to listen more than my one mouth to speak.

Years later (and wiser), I sat down with my wife and asked her: *If you want to feel loved by me, what would you like me to do?*

I also asked her four other questions regarding our relationship:

1. *What do I do that you want me to do more?*
2. *What do I do that you want me to do less?*
3. *What do I do that you want me to stop?*
4. *What don't I do that you want me to start doing?*

The answers to these five questions gave me the manual for making her feel loved and cared for.

Using this information and practicing what a weekly magazine called *daily sex*, we started to build a magical and loving marriage. *Daily sex* is you doing something **every day** for your partner, showing them you love him or her. It could be buying flowers or something as simple as a hug or a tender stroke of gratitude on the cheek.

For several years after the above incident, we were deep into personal development education and events. We wanted to learn as much as we could about relationships and success. A revolutionary experience was attending Tony Robbins UPW. I was an IT professional, and my wife was a teacher. We were living ordinary lives, not extravagant in any way, but we did not lack anything either.

One day, my wife, Ann-Charlotte, came home from the university she attended at the time and said she was going to become a certified coach. Said and done! We both became coaches in NLP (Neuro-Linguistic Programming) and ICF. And *this* probably saved our lives.

Let me tell you how.

In 2009, I worked as an IT professional, and my wife and I had tried to start up our coaching business for a long time, but without success. We needed additional income. So, just like our coaching colleague, we became a franchisee to his business partner. The business was in domestic services, gardening, construction, and corporate staffing. During the following two years, we ran our business and worked on building the brand. In 2011, we decided to either expand our business to new areas or quit since it didn't generate the income we wanted. We chose to expand. Little did I know that this was the start of several years of struggle, fights, and lawsuits.

During 2011, we were forced into a financial system created by the franchise owner. I immediately discovered that something was wrong, but I couldn't figure out what it was. Among the franchisees, I was alone to think so. I announced I didn't want to use the system since the franchise owner did not fix the errors. I was immediately threatened by a fine according to the franchise contract.

In early 2012, we found problems when doing the accounting for the entire year. There were *several* problems, and all the franchisees suffered because of them. Eight out of eleven franchisees wanted to leave the brand. Since my wife and I held on to the core value of always doing the right thing, we reported to the Swedish tax authorities the mistake of not paying enough taxes because of the errors in the franchise financial system. The tax authorities thanked us for our honesty and demanded that we pay the owed taxes in one month.

Having a business that barely kept us afloat, we couldn't pay the taxes owed. We borrowed substantial amounts of money from our parents to keep the business going, hoping that *someday* this business would give us the money to fulfill our dreams.

For eighteen months, we fought the authorities, but with no luck. Since we ran our company in a corporate form, that held us, as owners, personally liable for any debts. We knew it would only be a matter of time before the authorities sold our home at an executive auction. We also knew that we would only receive a fraction of the value if that happened, and we would still owe money to the tax authorities. Instead, we sold our home to pay the debts.

Our children, who had grown up in that home, spent their entire life in it, were devastated. At the ages of fifteen and seventeen, they blamed the authorities. We moved into my parents' large villa.

Because of the property sale, we now owed capital gains tax instead. We, and some of the other franchisees, bought ourselves out of the contract and started our own brand. Even though we loved the business and the services we provided, it never became the success we envisioned. From all the fights and lawsuits, we lost all passion for the business. In 2013, we wanted out!

In May 2016, we finally sold the business for a fraction of the company's worth. But we were free! Or so we thought.

When we sold the company, the new owners were to pay us for our assistance in helping them take over and refocus on new services. Three months later, they had turned great income streams into substantial debt for the company and wanted us to buy the company back as it was—debt and all.

Since I made the mistake of not canceling *all* the contracts our company had with suppliers and partners, on one contract, I was the responsible creditor for the invoices they sold.

So, the new owners used this, sold their invoices, and let me pay the invoicing company. They also bought luxury items in the company and could not cover the costs. Filing for their bankruptcy was our only option to stop bleeding money.

And there we were: company sold, no job, no income, and no unemployment benefit. We lived off the little money we had. It lasted a few months; then, we filed for help. We asked for social security contributions.

During the year we received this, we applied for many jobs but were always rejected. My wife and I were considered *too old, overqualified,* and *too entrepreneurial*. Amid our misery, the government withdrew their social security support with the motivation that we owned two dormant companies. Since this argument was against Swedish law, we sued the authorities . . . and lost.

During this time, the tax authorities also sent the Swedish bailiff authorities to seize the children's investment funds. Remember, we still had capital gains tax to pay. They took away the little money we had for survival, including the children's savings. This is the point our children decided not to trust the government ever again. Since the manner of seizure was illegal, of which the tax authorities were well aware, we sued the Swedish government and won.

But still, we had nothing to live on. I panicked, not knowing how to put food on the table for the following week. We had to borrow money from anyone who could help, including the grandparents' savings fund for our children. This was the lowest point of my life. I constantly dwelled on my misfortune and everything I couldn't do.

But as I said before, being a coach in business and personal development probably saved my life. I used this time to immerse myself in all the personal development education that I had collected. I discovered the *process of manifestation*, which tells us that all external results are first created internally in our minds.

I shifted my mindset from my situation, then, to the future of my dreams and desire. We focused on being grateful for what we had. We used the *Ultimate Success Formula*—rediscovering our purpose, creating visions, setting goals, and making plans. We continuously educated ourselves and attended every free seminar and event we could find. We made lots of new friends in the process.

One day, when taking a long walk with a close friend, he mentioned that one of his employees suddenly quit. I filled the position. It was part-time and low salary, but it meant the world to me. I started building my self-esteem again using my expertise, both as an IT professional and a coach. I could provide the necessities for my family.

A year later, I got a contract in my own company as a project manager for a large customer. From that day, in December 2019, my wife and I were able to slowly build on the magical vision we had for our future.

Today, we are continuously building the life of our joint vision. We use the active income that we receive to invest in our other projects, educational company, crypto, stocks, and properties, building our fortune. Today we receive (or find, if you will) new opportunities almost every day. We finally have the courage and strength to build the business of our passion, where we can assist others in changing their mindset, to create the magic of their dream lives.

For a long time, I held the franchise owner responsible for all the misfortune that hit us during those years. I don't anymore. I see it as something we needed to experience and learn to be able to fulfill our true purpose.

I am confident that what kept us going through all our setbacks and adversities was our continuous and massive love for each other and the people around us. Not to mention the willingness to trust that God, or the Universe, had something greater awaiting us in the future.

Together with personal development education, we were able to shift our mindset from the mess we created, from who we were before, to focus on our message and vision for tomorrow, based on who we are today.

## BIOGRAPHY

Being a lifelong problem-solver, Michael Wesley never quits! From the point of being broke, depressed, and desperate, with a deep and fiery passion, Michael now coaches and mentors people to grow their inner power, eliminate limitations, and create the life of their dreams and desires. As an entrepreneur, ICF and NLP coach, and a life strategist with a mindset that everything is achievable, Michael has an incredible gift for discovering solutions and structures to achieve desired outcomes while facing challenges. He uses his abilities to assist his clients in developing their ability to achieve amazing continuous successes on their path to excellence and mastery. He focuses his services on the three pillars needed in designing your freedom in life: health, wealth, and happiness. His passion is to see the excitement and fire in people's eyes as they discover their inner resourcefulness while creating amazing results in life.

Connect with Michael Wesley via https://wesleyenterprises.eu

CHAPTER 24

# Unwavering Determination And A Mother's Love

*By Mwansa Palangwa Gold*

There is nothing as beautiful as the African sunrise and its magnificent setting. My African story is as dynamic and exciting as that sun's path. While most people take an hour and a half to travel to South Africa from Zambia by air and forty-eight hours by road, it took me seven agonizing days on the road.

After my dad died, I asked my mom if I could move to South Africa to take advantage of a job opportunity so I could help her educate my four younger siblings. She agreed and arranged for me to stay with a family friend. The truth about our family ordeal was that we were too broke to afford a bus ticket to South Africa. My cousin, a cross-border truck driver, offered me a ride on his drive to Johannesburg. With all the border-crossing customs clearing procedures, the trip took an entire week. As I recall this experience, the words of Dan Rather come to mind: "If all difficulties were known at the outset of a long journey, most of us would never start out at all."[16]

On arriving in Johannesburg, I called a family friend to enquire about the possibility of hosting me. As fate would have it, she politely

---

16 "Dan Rather Quotes," BrainyQuote (Xplore), accessed April 23, 2021, https://www.brainyquote.com/quotes/dan_rather_387080.

informed me that I could not stay with her and further advised that I go back to Zambia.

My cousin was set to return to Zambia the following day. He told me if I did not have anywhere to stay, I would be better off going back with him. But I was determined to stay and succeed in South Africa.

A few hours before my cousin was to go back, I still had no place to stay. A childhood friend had given me his brother's and sister's number; they lived in Johannesburg. There was a chance of staying, and I was going to give it a shot. Out of utter desperation and sheer determination, I made the call and prayed for a miracle. God answered my prayers. I was picked up from the docking port, where I had spent my first two nights in Johannesburg, an hour before my cousin left. They graciously accommodated me, and to my great surprise, they knew another cousin of mine, Perry T., and my Uncle Chapi M., who also lived in Johannesburg. They later took me in.

**Tough Times, Toughens Up**

To say South Africa was tough and rough (IS an) understatement of the century.

I had my first encounter with homelessness and the evils of racism in South Africa. In search of a job as a waitress, I was brutally told they did not employ black girls and that not only was I black, but I was *very* black, and I would scare off the customers. I did not leave until they first gave me a job as a cleaner. I used to clean toilets and wash dishes. Eventually, I started waitressing and became one of their best waitresses. On the weekends, I sang to entertain the very customers they claimed I would scare off because of my dark skin. The customers loved me; they called me "Shirley," in honor of the legendary Gospel singer, Shirley Caesar.

Around the same time, I found myself homeless and in the dangerous streets of South Africa. Praise God for great friends. My friend, Pam, a boarder at Rhema House, would sneak me in during the night, and we'd leave very early in the morning so we would not be discovered. Pam helped me find a place which I shared with another great friend, Amwazia C. The first few weeks in our new place, we slept on the floor. Later, we raised enough money and bought a bed. How we rejoiced on the day the bed was delivered! The simple pleasures of life!

During these challenging times, never did I even entertain the thought of going back home. When I was afraid, which was quite often, I would summon my alter ego, "Mosi-oa-Tunya"—"The Smoke that Thunders." As Mosi-oa-Tunya, I was fearless! To quote the Legendary late Kobe Bryant: "If you see me in a fight with a bear, pray for the bear"[17] (#MambaMentality).

A few months later, another childhood friend of mine, the late Cecilia, introduced me to a powerful woman, Margo S. Margo gave me my first opportunity in the South African corporate world as a tea girl in Hillbrow, Johannesburg. All I needed was an entry into the corporate world, regardless of position. Tea girl was just fine by me. By the time I left that company, I was Assistant Executive Secretary to the CEO.

To South Africa, 'I came, I saw, and I conquered.' At the age of twenty-three, I was one of the youngest temp managers at Deloitte & Touché, heading a temp team in forensic investigation, information gathering, data capturing, and automation.

I believed if I could make it in post-apartheid South Africa as a young, black female and foreigner, I could make it anywhere in the world.

My friends, John M. and Suzio G., and I always joked that we graduated from Hillbrow University, the school of "Hard Knocks."

My dream and ultimate goal was to go to America. I was denied a US visa more times than I care to count. But I had unwavering determination, a praying mother, and her undying love by my side, and I kept going back until I was granted the visa. My best friend, Lontia, arranged for my mother to jump on the next bus from Zambia to Johannesburg, that very

---

17 "'If You See Me in a Fight with a Bear, Pray for the Bear.',," Kobe Bryant Quote, accessed April 23, 2021, https://quotefancy.com/quote/849272/Kobe-Bryant-If-you-see-me-in-a-fight-with-a-bear-pray-for-the-bear.

day, I got the visa. Glory to God! By this time, we had the money for a luxury bus.

In a few days, I left for America with my mother's blessings.

I am the "Smoke that Thunders." If any obstacle is in my way, I move it. If there is no path, I pave one for myself. And if I have no keys to a door, I blast through!

**Coming to America**

From being a manager at Deloitte and Touché, I was now an au pair to five kids in Columbus, Ohio. It was not easy (and that's putting it lightly). After a month, I found a great family in San Diego with two beautiful kids. My two-year-old charge became my best friend. Even if he could never pronounce my African name, Mwansa, he insisted on calling me by it.

In need of extra money to continue helping my mother and siblings back in Zambia, I started picking up used cans and bottles from trash cans. Before dawn, I would take my host mother's car and drive through the neighborhood streets to pick up cans and bottles and exchange them for a small fee at the recycling center. After working hours, I would go to the nearby community college I attended for a short period, picking up cans and bottles from as many trash cans I could before it got too dark. My host parent, Maggie, once asked me where I got my strong work ethic from? I don't recall giving her an answer, but I remember her telling me that I would one day become a millionaire with such determination.

During my spare time in San Diego, I attended conferences by Tony Robbins, who is my mentor and coach to this day, along with many others. It was during this time I was introduced to network marketing.

I want to take this moment and answer the question my host mom asked me many years ago. I get my backbone and fearlessness from very strong women in my life: my two mothers, Lovesness Palangwa and Rose Chabala; my many grandmothers; and countless aunties. Five very special women, in particular, have been very instrumental in teaching me how to navigate the complexities of society and the cooperate world: Ketty N., Margo S., Sampa K., Judy C., and Precious M. These women never allowed me to give up or stay down and beaten for too long. I have always been surrounded and supported by men and women of God, too many to mention. But these three have had a lasting impact on my life: Bishop Ruben Sambo, Bishi (Dr) Eddie Mulenga, and Pastor Stephen Biniyam. You see, I come as one, but I stand as a million.

From San Diego, I moved to Indianapolis, where I worked making and packing boxes in a warehouse. I found myself homeless for a second time, though this time, it was for one night only.

I started my career in information security in 2005. I have worked for companies like CNO Financial Groups, Navient, Rolls Royce under Capgemini, and Anthem Inc, to mention a few. I am a Certified Information Systems Auditor, a Cyber Security Analyst, and a Social Entrepreneur. My siblings, Victor P., Chanda P., Chomba P., Chalwe P., and Joseph P., have gone on to be Accountant/Businessman, Medical Professional, Bankers, and Engineer, respectively. Never give up fighting for the people you love and who love you back in equal measure, if not more. In the famous words of Vince Lombardi, "Winners never quit, and quitters never win."[18] Refuse to quit; there is more to your life.

In the same year, 2005, I got married. We moved to Boston, MA, the following year, where my ex-spouse was working on his MBA at Harvard Business School.

Those two years at Harvard Business School as a supporting spouse were my most brutal years in America thus far. I went into a deep depression, and my "loving" (sarcasm intended) husband signed me to a psychiatric hospital for a couple of days until the doctors determined I was in the wrong place, and all I needed was some medication for my depression. I gladly took these for two months and have never been on antidepressants ever since. I joyfully divorced him. Life will knock you down, and sometimes, if not many times, the very people you love will

---

18 "Vince Lombardi Quotes," BrainyQuote (Xplore), accessed April 23, 2021, https://www.brainyquote.com/quotes/vince_lombardi_122285.

disappoint you and betray you. Instead of blaming everyone and staying buried under the mess, get up and fight another round and then some.

I got remarried to Dr. Kennedy Mwacalimba, and together we have three lovely kids: Zahara, Takiyah, and Asher, famously known as the "ZTA Squad."

In America, to use Pitbull's artistic words: ". . . I saw, I conquered, I came."[19] I'm a fireball!

David Goggins, author of the best-selling book *Can't Hurt Me*, says, "I tell them where I come from to give them hope."[20] Echoing his words, I share my story to give hope, faith, and fierce determination to never stop dreaming and reaching for the moon (#Stayhard).

My story may be unique, but the lessons are universal. I want you to see through my eyes that no matter what life throws at you, you can always win if you choose to win.

**Chapter Action Points**

Two important takeaways from this chapter:
1. Have unwavering determination.
2. Fight for your dreams. Break the rules if you have to.

When life knocks you down, and I promise it will from time to time, get back up and fight for your dreams and those you love.

If the nay-sayers say, 'You can't have it' because of your heritage, the color of your skin, your gender, your education, or lack of it, prove them wrong. Get in the ring of life and fight like your life depends on it because it does! #GNQ, Giants Never Quit!

---

19 "Pitbull (Ft. John Ryan) – Fireball," Genius, July 23, 2014, https://genius.com/Pitbull-fireball-lyrics.
20 David Goggins, Can't Hurt Me: Master Your Mind and Defy the Odds (Anchorage, AK: Lioncrest Publishing, 2020).

## BIOGRAPHY

Mwansa Palangwa Gold has been working with the youth as Founder and President of the Africa Youth Social Entrepreneurs for over ten years. She inspires young people and helps them unlock their entrepreneurial potential. Her vast experience as a Certified Information Systems Auditor (CISA) and Cybersecurity Analyst beautifully finds expression in the way she sees the authentic self within people. Her mission is to inspire people to take deliberate, progressive action through self-development, self-education, develop self-confidence, become more resourceful, and open them to wealth-creation opportunities. She is also the Co-Founder and Chief Executive Officer of A&M Empowered.

Connect with Mwansa Gold via https://linktr.ee/Mwansa_Gold

CHAPTER 25

# God's Undeniable LOVE

*By Naquita Rae Rivas*

I grasped my dresser with my left hand, my body hunched over; I yelled in questioning agony, "Lord, what have I done?" I had never experienced so much physical pain. A couple of days prior, I had bent over to put on my sandals after a quick workout when a sharp, electrifying, stabbing pain pierced my lower back, crippling me. An immediate visit to the chiropractor and massage therapist did little to ease the intolerable discomfort. The enforced sitting on the couch had me restless; the urge to get up and do something productive only got me as far as my dresser.

I had lost function of my abdominal muscles, so I used a cane to get to my bedroom. The suffering reached my heart, my mind, and my ego. I finally humbled myself to ask the question of accountability: "What have I done?" Tears rolled down my face, and I sobbed as never before. It made the pain worse, but I did not care because I yearned for the truth. I did not hear an audible answer, as I never have, in all my believing life. At that moment, I understood my depression to a small degree, which humbled me even more. I fell to my knees and slowly positioned myself into a fetal position, continuing to cry. I kept asking, "Why am I alone? Why am I alone?" I didn't want anyone to see me in such pain. I knew deep down I did not want to ask for help. I only wanted someone to care. The self-pity took over amid the confusion. I had never felt so alone. Exhausted from the awful cry, I slowly sat up and leaned against the dresser. I wiped away the tears with my sleeve and took a deep breath in the hope of releasing the pain. Then, a heavy presence of peace covered me from head to toe. Indeed, I was not alone.

A year earlier, at the age of thirty, I weighed the heaviest in all my life. I justified the weight as a sign of aging. I told myself my body could handle the pounds, but something was not right. Then came the morning I could not hold up my arm when brushing my teeth—it was simply too heavy. A strong vibration raced through my shoulder, forcing me to put my arm down. I took a moment to rest and began again, but suddenly, I felt sore, tired, and very confused. I thought, 'I am only thirty. This is unacceptable!' This red flag prompted a deep concern for my health. The following year was a series of establishing doctors, joining weight-loss programs, and looking for an explanation as to why I was experiencing so much pain and fatigue. I felt I was a nuisance. Ultrasounds, MRIs, bloodwork, and hours of doctor consultations showed no apparent signs of the root pain, much less any reason why I should be concerned. Therefore, I did my best to continue physical therapy, eat better, help those around me, and stay active. It was essential for me to keep moving as much as possible. I was on my way to recovery. My mom, a personal trainer and health consultant, would periodically criticize my eating, drinking, and exercise form. To her, something was off. I was not moving correctly. My response to her was rarely well-received. Looking back now, I am embarrassed to have taken offense. She is my most valued guide for health and wellness. Just months after I was born, she started teaching aerobics and still helps others reach their fitness goals.

At sixteen, my mom introduced me to network marketing. She took my brother and me to a conference in San Diego, CA, to learn about liquid vitamins. Intrigued by the entrepreneur's training and mindset, I learned it is the "Why" that should motivate us. At an even earlier age, with my whole being, I knew the whole world needed to know about the love of Jesus Christ. The greatest gift my mom ever shared with me was to know the love of God and the ability to freely have a personal relationship with Him. The combination of faith and entrepreneurship set the stage for many awkward but wonderful conversations. I was always ready to proclaim the love of Jesus and possibly sell something. This passion allowed me to form some of the most genuine, long-lasting relationships.

However, throughout the years, a part of me was unwilling to do the work—the studying, the discipline, the numbers—I would simply "try." I became increasingly bitter and angry because I felt unsuccessful in achieving my goals. I had experienced many traumatic car accidents and struggled to recover properly. This discouraged me from being involved in activities I loved. There was always a lingering pain disconnecting my mind from my body. At the age of eighteen, I attempted to study dance at the University of Colorado in Boulder. My very first dance class was at CU Boulder in the glorious lower dance studio with women who had been dancing since childhood. Optimistic, I forged through the vigorous art, hoping I could one day learn enough to teach, but somehow the pain in my body distracted me from dance. I struggled with learning the choreography, aesthetics, and proper form.

In my third year at CU Boulder, a teacher suggested I choose a different major. I grabbed my things from my locker and never went back. I was heartbroken. I let her convince me I was not good enough. Looking back, I realize pain and offense held me back from doing many things. Many years later, I started to reflect on all my past failures. I gained the wisdom of the mind, body, and spirit connection, much like Father, Son, and Holy Spirit—all separate, but all one. I uncovered some deep-rooted sources which had been overlooked and unresolved throughout my life. One was a broken hip from a car accident at the age of seventeen. I'm almost positive the rest of my issues were emotional trauma. At times my mind just wouldn't let my body do what it was created to do and sometimes vice-versa. Can you relate?

Between the ages of seventeen to thirty, I held onto all these traumas and tried to ignore my hurt. Then, a miracle happened: I crashed. My body, mind, and soul could not take it anymore. You might say the electrifying pain in my back made me realize my purpose. Feeling the Shalom (Peace) of God as I leaned up against my dresser, I silenced my mind long enough to ask God, "Please heal my heart." I took responsibility for my crusty attitude and began the journey of forgiveness. Rather than compare myself to others, I began to forgive myself for all the self-pity and misunderstandings, for all the hurt I had caused others through my ugly perception of them, and mostly, for not knowing how God views me and all his children. He loves us!

I let go of all the yesterdays, the exercise I did not do, the junk food I put in my mouth, and the money I foolishly spent. I surrendered it all; I began to heal immediately. Yes, God's love heals immediately. I was able to stand and find a place to rest in God's undeniable love—a love so overwhelming. David, the author of Psalms, explains it so sweetly. "Oh Lord, you have examined my heart and know everything about me. You know when I sit down or stand up. You know my thoughts even when I am far away. You see me when I travel and when I rest at home. You know everything I do. You know what I am going to say even before I say it, Lord. You go before me and follow me. You place your hand of blessing on my head. Such knowledge is too wonderful for me, too great for me to understand! You made all the delicate, inner parts of my body and knitted me together in my mother's womb. You saw me before I was born. How precious are your thoughts about me, O God. They cannot be numbered! I can't even count them; they outnumber the grains of sand! And when I wake up, you are still with me" (Psalms 139:1-18 NLT). This love is so pure. How awesome, the God of all creation pursues us, thinks of us, and knows us. He is a God who does not need us but wants us.

I know I am not perfect; God knows none of us can be good. For this purpose, He sent Jesus. What great news! "For God so loved the world, that He gave his only begotten Son, that whosoever believeth in Him, should not perish, but have everlasting life. For God sent not His Son into the world to condemn the world; but that the world through Him might be saved" (John 3:16-17 KJV). When I asked Jesus Christ, the Son of God, into my heart, my life changed. It is not about religion; it is about a personal relationship with our Creator. It is about being vulnerable and confessing our hearts' aches and joys. In this, we can have intimacy with Yeshua, our God, who undeniably loves us. As we move into uncertain times in this world, it gives me great joy to know God has my back. He says, "Call unto me, and I will answer thee, and shew thee great and mighty things, which thou knowest not" (Jeremiah 33:3 KJV). I have called unto Jesus, and He has answered. He is my friend, my mentor, and my focus when the pain of the world, or simply just the pain in my body, is overwhelming. He is with me; He is with us! "For I am persuaded, that neither death, nor life, nor angels, nor principalities, nor powers, nor things present, nor things to come, nor height, nor depth, nor any other creature, shall be able to separate us from the love of God, which is in Jesus Christ our Lord" (Romans 8:38-39 KJV).

If, for some reason, you do not know Jesus Christ as your personal Lord and Savior, I invite you to pray with me:

Lord Jesus, I know the sacrifice you made for me. You paid the price for my sins, and I ask Your forgiveness. Live in my heart. Be a part of my daily life, reveal yourself to me, and fill me with your everlasting love, peace, and joy! Change me, renew me, heal me, in Your Holy Name, Amen!

I am filled with so much joy knowing you have heard the gospel of Jesus Christ. It has been the saving grace in my life. I am confident it will change your life. Please reach out to me or other believers in Yeshua for prayer and fellowship. I look forward to hearing your testimony. I will leave you with one last word: "And we know that all things work together for good to them that love God, to them who are called according to his purpose" (Romans 8:28). I pray these scriptures will touch your heart, stir your soul, and bring you closer to your purpose in Christ Jesus. Amen.

# BIOGRAPHY

Naquita Rae Rivas is a successful business owner and entrepreneur from Pagosa Springs, Colorado. She has a passion for health and wellness. She attributes her healthy habits and desire to learn to her mother, June. As a professional cosmetologist, Naquita is learning the art of listening to peoples' deepest secrets, dreams, goals, beliefs, and opinions while transforming their hair, nails, and self-confidence. Naquita loves to travel and is an alumnus of the non-profit organization Up With People. She was also a contestant on the game show The Price Is Right, where she won a trip to Iceland and traveled with her best friend, Tia Eleanor. Her Tia Edna has taught her about God's undeniable love and has encouraged her outgoing, fun-loving attitude. Naquita is convinced every individual, who has walked into her life, has made a significant impact. These divine relationships have made her more compassionate, empathic, and loving. She gives all the glory to her loving Abba Father.

Connect with Naquita Rae Rivas via https://linktr.ee/naquitaraerivas

CHAPTER 26

# A Paradoxical Paradox

*By Oluwafunmike Ani*

"If you will not fight for right when you can easily win without bloodshed; if you will not fight when your victory is sure and not too costly; you may come to the moment when you will have to fight with all the odds against you and only a precarious chance of survival. There may even be a worse case. You may have to fight when there is no hope of victory, because it is better to perish than to live as slaves."[21]—Winston Churchill.

It was 10 am, on January 08, 1982. I was amid the hustle and bustle preceding the annual matriculation ceremony at my alma mater. I was getting dressed, posing for pictures, showcasing the matric gown, and having a swell time because I was proud to have scaled all hurdles to be accepted into that university to study medicine. Exhilarating, right? Yes, but not for me! That was probably the saddest day of my life! You see, I was just going through the motions and keeping appearances while unsure of what to do with my non-cheery discovery. An unexpected pregnancy was in progress, and the guy responsible was not interested in becoming a father!

For a girl raised by highly religious parents (my mum was a deaconess and my dad a strong church leader), decorum demanded that at least a

---

21  "Top 24 Winston Churchill Quotes to Inspire You to Never Surrender," Goalcast, April 12, 2021, https://www.goalcast.com/2017/06/20/top-24-winston-churchill-quotes-to-inspire-you-to-never-surrender/.

marriage be quickly transacted to mitigate the associated shame. But alas! There would not be one as far as the unfolding events revealed. A typical conversation between my guy and his friends went like this: *'Are you the father?' 'Yes, of course.' 'Is there a reason she would not be the right wife for you?' 'None, she had been so kind to me, but I just am not ready for this!' 'Don't you think you need to wake up to reality? You are approaching forty already!' 'Stop the pressure, please! If she is so special to you, maybe you should marry her instead?'*

Devastated, crushed, silenced, a usually bubbling social butterfly transformed into a moody, unsure, depressed version of herself! Not sure where to turn, I quickly became a recluse.

My supposed best-friend-for-life, in whom I had confided, deserted me in a hurry and even accused me of being a hypocrite! The worst part was that we were roommates at the residential hall—a plan we both hatched as best friends, but now so incongruent! Just how does a newly registered undergraduate deal with so much so soon and so suddenly? My trusted mate and lover of several months now turned into a cold-hearted fellow who preferred funding the abortion of our love consequence, claiming financial inability to give the baby its right to life! The pressure to terminate was so irritating that I had to do the needful: cut off from the ensuing unhealthy relationship. It was enough to be betrayed but intolerable to be insulted and treated like an idiot! I was not having any of it. All my life, there was a level of insult I would never justify.

An army of tyrannical thoughts so torrential swallowed me that damning them was impossible. What should I do? Comply with the termination demand or what? To be clear, I was not a novice with pregnancy removals, having had a few for some inexplicable reasons. I was fed up with the whole experience. It was expensive (if done by an experienced hand in a safe environment) and involved a great deal of pain, non-synced bleeding, emotional turmoil, a period of inactivity and more… It was at this point that I toyed with some destructive ideas like suicide, running far away till the baby was born, reaching out to the father's parents to house me during the pregnancy, and collect the child after delivery so I could return and pick my life up from where I left off. Facing my parents with these matters was just a "mission impossible" for me.

This turmoil went on for days that turned into weeks, and the almighty morning sickness ensured I could not effectively attend lectures or undertake the practical sessions. In anger, I went to see my abortion specialist, but he too acted reluctantly and was not too pleased with me for the first time! Instead of an instant session, he set an appointment for six hours in advance that turned out to be the means of my deliverance from whatsoever was to go wrong with the upcoming procedure! I Immediately exited the facility, flagged down a public van, and was lucky to get a seat for my journey back to campus. As soon as I settled in the bus, the inexplicable began; huge rivers of tears started running down my eyes with huge sobs freely emitting from my inner being. It was scary and uncontrollable. There I was, feeling so embarrassed in public, a confirmed babe like me! I felt agitated with the whole experience. A fresh tirade of self-questioning followed: What is happening to me? Why this teary fountain? What kind of a child am I carrying? Could this be the child bemoaning its impending demise? It was beyond understanding, stranger than fiction, as the saying goes. This teary drama lasted about ten minutes, and in a flash, I realized I would not be returning to that facility, not in six hours, not twenty-four, not ever again. I suddenly fell in love with the living one in my womb, denounced the consequences, and chose to handle my fate. To my shock, the teary fountain instantly ceased gushing, and great peace washed over my soul. I could still hear myself speaking to my unexpected and rejected child while still on the bus ride: "Hey baby! Together, you and I will find a way. I will figure it out; somehow, we will survive." And that sealed my resolve. All I needed to do first was to burn the bridge so I could be at peace.

I instantly headed for the telephone room, called Mr. Loverboy, and made my warrior decision clear: TO KEEP MY BABY, NEVER EXPECTING A DIME FROM HIM. This also meant, in the future, his baby could be traced to the bin of the abortion clinic he had envisioned. What became of a jobless, struggling girl from middle-lower-class parents? She enrolled for a five-year course of intensive studies in a prestigious medical college. To take such an extreme decision defied all my understanding! I was so angry at the unfairness of it all that I resolved to succeed against all odds to properly raise a child, giving whatever it took. Oh boy!

So, I had to instantly set my survival agenda in motion.

My attitude had always synced with Winston Churchill's saying: "The price of greatness is responsibility."[22] Therefore, my first line of action was a visit to the student affairs office to "report myself" and figure out which way to turn. I was so determined to succeed as a single but faithful mum to my unborn child. Even the possibility of losing my undergraduate degree could not deter my decision. Thank God, the officer had good news for me that the system saw all students as adults running their private life, so no repercussions were expected. He was more concerned about my ability to cope with the intensive course content of medical studies. His kindness was the first sip of cool water to my bewildered soul.

The next task was breaking the news to my parents and to extended family, who were full of puritanical views and stereotypes. But this would be unavoidable!

Being a daddy's girl all my life, I grew up in an atmosphere of mutual emotional distance from my mum. You rightly guessed who got to know first. Dad returned from his usual weekend trips to our hometown only to meet a slip of paper under the door of his room, informing him of the crisis. It was beyond me to have a one on one! To my surprise, I did not see the expected hell-let-loose response! It seemed the Merciful One had allowed a soft landing! Whether it was the fact that a few months earlier, we lost one of my cousins to complications from an unwholesome abortion that made dad so calm in his response and acceptance of an 'addition' to his children, I will never know (he died before I could be healed

---

22 "Reimagining Our Future," Reimagining Our Future, May 5, 2015, https://reimaginingourfuture.org/the-price-of-greatness-is-responsibility-winston-churchill/#:~:text=%E2%80%9CThe%20price%20of%20greatness%20is%20responsibility%E2%80%9D%20%E2%80%94%20Winston%20Churchill.

enough to engage him on this). But such was his response: taking instant responsibility to support his special daughter during her dark moments, knowing that tongues would wag, and the church might discipline them for poor parenting. But that never deterred him. In his words: "Anger is a wrong response to increase." This was in February 1982! Nevertheless, he summoned Mr. Loverboy for a meeting, the outcome of which was so unsavoury. Dad forbade him from being within 100 km of our residence upon threat of bodily harm! This meant an added responsibility to fund my antenatal bills, apart from my educational bills, ferry me for my antenatal visits, be available for day-care, and future school runs for his grandson. No wonder the two were deeply bonded. Grandpa's early demise remained too painful to forget!

Life never returned to normal. Poor self-acceptance put me in a state of low self-esteem for several years, despite strongly focusing on my studies. On February 13, the same year, I met some One who said, "Come unto me, all ye that labour and are heavy laden, and I will give you rest. Take my yoke upon you and learn of me; for I am meek and lowly in heart: and ye shall find rest unto your souls. For my yoke is easy, and my burden is light" (Matthew 11:28-30). I committed my all to Him, left the driver seat of my life to Him while I became His passenger. This transformed my life values to such a degree that even dad would not fault the perceived fanaticism associated with the born-again 'sect' of those days.

Being raised in a highly religious home by less perfect but sanctimonious parents and relatives had its effect on my religious attitudes as a young adult. Discovering that the preacher often lived a life inconsistent with the doctrines he preached contributed to my frequent engagement in disruptive behaviour that separated me from the clan. Sure enough, only dad was sympathetic to my plight. Other relatives felt embarrassed and hatched a plan to withdraw me from my studies so I would be a futureless ex-medical student! A punishment for humiliating the clan. But the outcome of my initial preposterous trip to the student affairs office on that epiphany day became that which saved my future as an MD from the hatchet of vengeance!

I remained true to my resolution, focused only on the agenda to raise a great son, walked with my Lord daily, and succeed in my studies, despite the realities of financial deprivation and fear of friendships. What helped me succeed was the relationship I forged with the Nazarene who spilled His blood that I may be free to live without condemnation, and the support of dad, who sacrificed his pride that I might succeed despite my unadvised adventures.

All my life, before accepting the eternal love of the Nazarene, the quote I acquired as an avid reader of literature in my childhood was my clarion call: "For it is not life that matters, but the courage, fortitude, and determination you bring to it."[23] Growing up, there were many situations ready to crush the spirit. But for this one quote, I could not have blazed through.

A testimony to my transformation was that I eventually found love again and got married within few months of graduating from med school, five years later. The wedding ceremony was so elaborate that the whole city wondered, "Who is this bride?" It was reward-time for my precious dad. My parents unexpectedly became sermon topics for how parents should never give up but love and believe in their children, even though they be non-conforming! A paradoxical paradox!

## BIOGRAPHY

Oluwafunmike Ani, a community ophthalmologist, spent the last three decades delivering eye care to the marginalized of society, extending beyond her native Nigeria to India, Togo, and Liberia. Between 2008–2009, she headed the Phebe Hospital Eye Care Program in Gbanga, Liberia, delivering hundreds of eye surgeries, rejigging several eye care systems destroyed during the war, and was regular guest at the Curtinton

---

23  "A Quote by Muhammad Ali Jinnah," Goodreads, accessed April 15, 2021, https://www.goodreads.com/quotes/457291-you-will-have-to-make-up-for-the-smallness-of.

University radio program "Guides To Good Health." A mother at heart, she worked tirelessly with the children and adolescent arm of the Bethel World Outreach Church branch and is fondly called "mother of children." An ex-chairman of the Public Health Group of the Ophthalmological Society of Nigeria and Executive Producer of an edutainment movie "Avoidable Blunder" (a behaviour change communication tool), she tackles pervasive societal ignorance and assists those with treatable blindness in low-income areas.

Connect with Oluwafunmike Ani via https://linktr.ee/Oluwafunmike

CHAPTER 27

# Inner Conflict

*By Shaun Bass*

Have you ever asked yourself: "How do I get out of my own way?" Better yet, have you ever wondered what's holding you back? These are the kinds of thoughts most people keep to themselves. They dance around in the back of our minds as we put on a smile for the world! As you read this, you will realize that you are not alone anymore and that others struggle with their inner conflict as well.

Hello, I'm Shaun Bass. To give you an insight as to why I asked myself those questions, I'm going to share some of my life with you, hoping that we are relatable and I can help. I grew up in a lower, financially blue-collar family. I say 'financially' because nothing else about my family was "blue-collar." I come from a large group of people who would give someone the shirt off their back or their bottom dollar to help them in need, and that's an elite status in my book! Growing up with such influences taught me many things, much of which I didn't understand until my late teens and early twenties. I'll never forget my dad telling me: "Son, you'll understand when you're older." Of course, that was the answer to a lot of my questions. As I grew, that statement, along with many others, taught me humility and patience. Having little to no money helped with that, and I'm not saying that to make anyone feel sorry for me. I never went without the necessities of life: ramen noodles, water to boil them in, and southern sweet tea! I'm just kidding. I was well-fed, and I knew, from a young age, that I had it a lot better than most kids my age. My parents divorced when I was two, so I always had twice as many birthdays and Christmases, and as awesome as that was for me, I despised the fact that I had to bounce back and forth between my mother and father. At that time, I felt like I was in a broken or split family. For years, I told myself that I would never put my kids through that. I believe that was my first inner conflict. Do I hate this situation, or do I embrace it? Once again, my father's words were true, and as I grew older, I understood that there was nothing split or broken about it; I simply gained an even bigger family! They say, "It takes a village to raise a child." Well, I definitely had a village!

It took years to learn this lesson, and I was so young, I didn't even realize I was learning to always look at the bright or positive side of any situation. And I felt that having such a large, loving family helped me grow into this mindset as a kid. Now that I've learned about the Personal Development industry, I understand that anyone can develop this trait—loving family or not. It's something you can do right by yourself, but you'll have to consistently practice it until it becomes a subconscious habit. So here I am, a young adult with an optimistic outlook on life, just living for the weekend, as is the same for a lot of you, I'm sure. At that point in life, my only inner conflict was: 'How am I going to pay for this?' 'This' being either fixing my truck when it broke down or a boat, ATV, or vacation trip I wanted to purchase but couldn't afford. So, I did all that I knew to do: work more hours and find a higher-paying job. After switching jobs a few times, I realized that I enjoyed going to work—at first, anyways. At the beginning of each job, I was eager to get out of bed and trade my time for money, but then six months to a year later, it would become irritating. I would drag myself out of bed and be in a kind of bleak mood. Then, I'd find a better job; maybe it paid more, or maybe it was just more interesting. But once again, six months to a year after, that wouldn't matter, and I'd start resenting having to go to work. The newness of each job was just a distraction from my real issue.

It's funny how you can hear or read the exact words time and time again, but one day, they just click inside your mind! Maybe it's because of the mood you are in when you read them or the tone of voice in which you hear them. I knew that not everyone had to ask for time off work. I knew that not everyone spent more time at work than they did with their family and friends. I read and heard about these kinds of people. It was only after a friend introduced me to some of her new friends that I truly realized that I didn't have to ask for time off. I didn't have to spend more time at a job than I did with family and friends! After being around and learning from my newfound friends, I figured out my issue: I hated not being my own boss! I did not like the idea of being told when I was allowed to go on vacation or having to ask if I could take off early so I could get something done during business hours. I wanted to be able to do what I wanted, when I wanted, for however long I wanted. Those were some of the things that dragged me down at work. So now, I knew I had to get out of the rat race one way or another. There I was, in my mid-twenties, realizing an inner conflict: how do I get out of the employee lifestyle and find a way to have both time and money freedom? Sure, I could open up my own mechanic shop, but that would only potentially bring me more money but would surely take up much more of my time. Or I could sell everything I own and live off-grid, which would give me plenty of time but no money to do the things I'd like to do.

My new friends who helped me understand the issue I was having with jobs also chimed in with a solution. They were a part of an industry that allowed everyday, average people to obtain the kind of lifestyle I was after. Of course, I jumped on board with them, not having a clue as to what I was getting into. Sheer excitement carried me through this venture for a while. I had lifelong friends join me, and we had a great time meeting new people and seeing new places. It even led us Florida boys up north to see snow for the first time, and those are memories I'll get to share with my grandchildren! After some time, things began to fade. What we had built slowly began crumbling, and no one seemed to care. I think it was because we didn't truly understand what we had gotten our hands into, and even though I knew it was my way out, I did nothing. It was frustrating to know that all I had to do was a few simple things consistently to continue on the path I told myself I wanted to be on, yet I didn't. I didn't have to "tell myself" at the beginning of this adventure because I knew, without a doubt, that this opportunity hit the nail on the head for me. It was literally my dream coming true! But after watching it all fall apart and seeing how I reacted towards it, it made me think: 'Is this what I truly wanted? If this is truly what I desired, I would have moved mountains to make it happen, right?' I beat myself up for quite some time. Thoughts of going in a different direction or just giving up would always be crossing my mind. I knew for sure that all other business ventures would not be able to get me to my goal. So, I kept trying to pull myself out of this negative slump that was getting me nowhere. Every day, I wondered how I could better myself and grow into the person I needed to be to reach my goal. After reading books and attending personal development seminars, I felt I had a grip on what I needed to do.

Have you ever been in a situation where you thought about something daily, and yet for some reason, simply didn't act on those thoughts at all? After consuming more books, audios, and inspirational videos, I came across a book by Nick Hall titled *I Know What to Do, So Why Don't I Do It?* As soon as I saw it, I said: 'That's me!' While almost everything else I read helped one way or another, this book really struck me. I can't say everything in it pertained to my specific issue, but reading everything he had to say was well worth it and entertaining.

This was the daily battle in my head: 'I know where I want to be in life, and I know the steps I need to take, so why am I not taking them?' There are, of course, many different struggles that people deal with inside their heads. Your conflict might be figuring out if moving away from family for a great promotion opportunity is the right choice, or do I stay in this toxic relationship for the children? Maybe you're not sure that it's worth divorcing your husband so you can hopefully marry your boyfriend. That's not it, but I'm sure someone is going through that battle in their head. A significant inner conflict that many people face, brought to light by many films, is whether or not they might be homosexual. Issues like these are the ones most people keep tucked away in their minds, and it haunts them at night when they try to sleep. This is emotionally stressful and unhealthy, and as hard as it may seem to simply open up to someone that will truly listen, it can ease the constant war inside your head. That statement I just made, most of you have heard time and time again in some form or fashion. I hope that I've worded it in a manner that strikes a nerve and helps you release some of your inner turmoil, or at least, take a step in the right direction. I wish I could promise you that once you've overcome one battle, there will never be another. But I simply don't believe that. I do believe, like so many other things in life, that the first step is the hardest. But once you've conquered it, the steps get easier and easier until you no longer worry about the next.

I can't tell you that all you have to do is this or that, and your inner conflict will disappear, though I wish I could. However, I can tell you that surrounding yourself with the right like-minded people works wonders on many levels. Always focus on the bright side of things, and be the positive person in a room full of gloom. In writing this, I've realized that I have yet another battle to face with myself, and the reason for writing this was to hopefully overcome another. It just goes to show that the fight never ends. So in the words of Sir Joseph Dirt: "You gotta keep on keepin' on."[24] If you keep reading and listening to people who empower you along every baby step towards your goals, the things you stress so heavily over will fall short, soon to be forgotten altogether.

---

24  Theresa Edwards, "You Guys, Joe Dirt Was so Wise, and These 7 Quotes Prove It," SheKnows, July 10, 2018, https://www.sheknows.com/entertainment/articles/1057887/life-advice-from-joe-dirt-that-is-surprisingly-spot-on/.

# BIOGRAPHY

Shaun Bass is a mechanic, heavy equipment operator, and networker. With a high school diploma and a few semesters of community college under his belt, he plans to help people in any way he possibly can. He understands that in order to do so, he must continually grow himself. Shaun keeps an open mind with a willingness to learn.

Connect with Shaun Bass via https://linktr.ee/shaunb30

CHAPTER 28

# Whatever It Takes

*By Sinan Abu-Aisheh*

Who would've thought that a young man from a broken family and addicted to heavy drugs would come out not only alive but thrive while impacting the lives of tens of thousands of people globally? Welcome to my story.

After my parents' divorce, I found myself lost, associating with the wrong crowds, and on the wrong side of the law. Fast forward, and things reached a point where I had gone deep enough that I thought my life was over and I wouldn't amount to anything. Irresponsible, depressed, lonely, and angry, I wanted to take it out on the world. Nothing I did was working. I knew I had the potential, but doubt was killing me inside. Until, one day, I had enough. *I read a book.* I attended a leadership seminar from which I was removed due to lack of participation. I was rough around the edges, but only I knew how badly I wanted to change.

My past and my addictions held me back. I finally realised that if I wanted to eliminate negative habits, positive habits needed to take their place. And until the pain of staying the same became greater than the pain of change, I wasn't ready to change. One day, after attending another leadership seminar, a lightbulb went on. Hope was reignited.

*I read my second book.* I got involved in a business that I had been resisting for years, and that one decision changed my life *forever*. I became a student of success, completely coachable. I was sick and tired of being sick and tired, so I put all my energy into bettering myself rather than hating my present and regretting my past.

Almost nine years later, and I'm thirty-one. I am the proud father of four beautiful children we had in four years, and I'm happily married to my wife, Angelik. I have a circle of amazing, loyal friends. The mentors with whom I surround myself daily are worth in the billions. I've built teams of over 2,000 people with tens of thousands of customers, and I've generated tens of millions in revenue in business so far and growing. I've been featured in our company success magazines multiple times, and I've spoken in front of crowds totalling around 100,000 people so far. I'm now a mentor to thousands, and I'm grateful every day for the opportunity to create an impact. Needless to say, I'm truly happy and content. Why am I telling you this? How did all of this happen? I decided to do *whatever it takes*. You can too. That's why I wrote this chapter: to serve you.

A few principles changed my life forever. After coaching them for years and having a deep passion to work on myself to model these principles, I have hoped for years that my story would inspire others around the world.

### *The Growth Journey*

You can't stop a decided man from a decided mission. I didn't want to be a failure anymore. I felt like it was my last chance to win. Everything I tried wasn't working because I hadn't filled my void of addictions with new habits and positive associations. I needed to immerse myself in an environment that normalised success to reprogram my mind and make winning normal. A total transformation was needed—a paradigm shift. My mentor always said, "Commitment is doing the thing you said you would do, long after the mood you said it in has left you." I was committed. No matter how I felt on bad days, I showed up.

I attended every training, *read more books*, and listened to motivational messages. I started setting goals and surrounded myself with those who achieved goals similar to what I wanted. I started building teams of people who also wanted to change their lives. My associations became more positive. I learnt that the growth journey is exciting and painful, but things hurt more when you're only half in. I was all in. People mocked and laughed at me as if I was delusional.

There's no trying when it comes to winning BIG. Trying means you'll do it until it becomes inconvenient. You have to do *whatever it takes*. You have to change your belief system. Your subconscious mind, which controls most of your life, needs adjusting; this takes time and effort. You're best thinking got you to where you're at today. You need new beliefs and thoughts to help you advance to a new level. That's why you must do *whatever it takes*. It's the only way you force yourself to stretch. And when you stretch consistently, you'll look back in awe at how far you've come.

What you focus on grows. When I focused on the negativity in my life, all I attracted was negativity. This time I had a desire to grow myself into my dreams. It's impossible to grow without working on something that challenges you. Growth comes after handling more pain than you thought you could. You have to be willing to live a few years like others aren't, so you can live the rest of your lives in ways they can't. I quit everything before this. But I realised: if I didn't sacrifice for what I wanted, what I wanted would've become the sacrifice.

I worked extremely hard. I became radical about my dreams. I had no idea what I was doing in the beginning. But imperfect-consistent work is better than perfect-inconsistent work. I've never met a fit person who didn't work out. I've never met a graduate who didn't pass their exams. I've never met a mother who didn't give birth. I've never met a successful businessperson without a history of hard work. Work ethic is essential. Most people want the prize, but they're not willing to pay the price. They want freedom, but they won't commit to the actions that'll set them free. I was willing to get uncomfortable for a few years so I could live comfortably for the rest of my life. Success and convenience have never been friends. I wasn't going to be blind to that fact.

No one's ever achieved their dreams by accident. And to achieve goals, you need to have goals! You can't go where you can't see! A traveller without a map will struggle to find their destination. Likewise, someone going for their dreams without clear goals will experience the same struggle. You become what you think about the most. This is what I learnt in the first two years of my journey. A self-made millionaire is just an average person who got obsessed and focused on specific goals and mastered skills that generated money. There's nothing special about them. They were just patient, disciplined, and relentless in their pursuit of success. Well, I guess that does make them special.

Most people fear rejection, change, failure, success, and the unknown. But when you keep avoiding fear, your success and dreams will disappear. You can fear flights, although you'll never experience the joys of travel. You can fear birth pains, but you'll never experience the blessings of motherhood. You can fear heartbreak, but you'll never experience true love. You can fear rejection and failure, but then you'll never experience success or ever truly live. Life's an adventure. Don't run from it. Embrace it.

Success in entrepreneurship is mostly emotional toughness. The disappointments can weigh you down, or you can strengthen yourself through them. You need strategy and a big reason *why* to keep you from quitting. It's going to get tough. If it was that easy, wouldn't everybody do it? Why don't they? Because they can't stand the struggle, pain, challenges, loneliness, empty bank accounts, betrayals, and the dark winters when everything crashes down. It happens to everyone. Either we quit and become mediocre, or we ride the wave and enjoy a life of freedom, adventure, love, growth, happiness, and choices. In the end, it's all worth it. Living full and dying empty, not living empty and dying full. It takes courage to design your life and become who you were born to be.

Emotions can make your life a living hell or a living heaven. The bridge to cross is tough, but it's achievable through personal responsibility, achievement, growth, and gratitude. You're either a slave or master to your emotions. One side equals failure, while the other equals success. Many people make permanent decisions from temporary problems. They choose their feelings over success when in reality, it's success that gives you the best feelings. Yes, people will let you down, but it's all about perspective. When people break their word, they're really just hurting their own integrity. If you could time-travel to the future and see that everything you're going through right now is just a part of the process of your eventual success, how would you work, feel, and operate today? I'm telling you from experience, marry the process and divorce the outcome. It's only tough until it becomes easy. It gets easier when you get better. Like the gym, when you train your muscles, you rip them, then they repair bigger and stronger. Avoiding pain is avoiding growth and strength.

Two years into my success journey, I went full-time with my online business. Four years in, we walked Angelik away from a law career she was pursuing. We had a family and plenty of time freedom. Life was great. The results showed from the sacrifices we made. We chose where we wanted to live, how to live, who to associate with, and how many days we wanted to work in a year. The results inspired others.

What keeps me ticking after eight years into my journey? I'm extremely passionate about growing leaders around the world who will serve and lead others. We found our platform to impact others, and we're committed to our mission. A selfish life is a pointless life. We're community people, and creating impact will make us happier than dollars ever will. The money rewards are great. We'll take that! You attract money when you add value to the marketplace anyway. But it's the impact that'll make your movement exhilarating. When you have so much to give, you won't be fulfilled unless you pour out what's in you into the world and make a difference.

### *Final Thoughts*

Everybody is searching for the answer. The answer lies in the book you haven't read, the training you didn't attend, the experiences you didn't learn from, and the prayer you haven't made. The answers are all there. You just have to be ready to internalise the information and apply it. When the student is ready, the teacher will appear.

We all love happy endings. But there's no such thing as a happy ending if there's no drama in the story. Work through the drama and never give up. There's joy in the journey, and there will be a happy ending if you don't quit.

I'm successful not because I didn't have pain and struggle, but because I had so much pain and struggle that I transformed into strength. Look at the rock that withstood pressure causing it to turn into a diamond. We're all the same. We have challenges and weaknesses. The difference is that successful people feel all of that but persist with vigour. That's why they say there's no traffic on the extra mile. There really isn't because not many dare go beyond the pain. All the treasures of life are on the other side of fear and pain.

Go and bless a life, and your life will be blessed. Change a life, and your life will change. Help others, and you'll be helping yourself. Love others, and love will find you. Sacrifice for others, and others will sacrifice for you. Be real with others, and others will be real with you. It all starts with YOU. You are the designer and architect of how this world treats you by what you put into the world. You reap what you sow—good or bad.

No matter how many challenges you face on your journey, promise yourself that you'll do *whatever it takes*. Imagine coming home to your family knowing that you *could* have, but you *didn't*. Or imagine going home to your family knowing that you *could* have, and you **DID**. Don't live in regret.

Finally, because books and people empowered me, I commit to empowering others through my *future books*.

Dear friends, don't forget you're here for a reason. Get out there and make this your season. Never let anyone convince you to stop dreaming. And work passionately on something that you believe in.


Yours truly,

Sinan Abu-Aisheh

# BIOGRAPHY

Sinan is a highly accomplished and renowned entrepreneur, business coach, and motivational speaker with his power of influence spanning global networks. His insightful business practices, management, and ethos are largely attributed to over eight years of intense practical experience, making him an authoritative force and a vital asset in business development, public speaking, and high-performance coaching. His affinity and expertise in global expansion, protocols, and networking have empowered him to culminate to the highest echelons of seniority, and his business acumen in a multi-billion-dollar industry has impacted countless lives. Sinan has authored a variety of courses through which many entrepreneurs have derived immense benefits. As Sinan's insatiable hunger for creating an impact is prodigious, he has embarked in studies within the field of Neuroscience, which certifies him as a Neuro-Change Master Trainer. You can find some of Sinan's trainings on YouTube and Vimeo.

Connect with Sinan Abu-Aisheh via https://linktr.ee/SinanAbuAisheh

CHAPTER 29

# The Other Side Of Forgiveness

*By Stephanie Woodley*

I grew up in a healthy family. My parents were hard-working people; my dad worked as a long-distance truck driver, while my mother was a nurse. I am the youngest child of seven siblings. I had two parents until my father passed away when I was ten years old. I remember my parents were always loving and affectionate to one another. They showed me a healthy example of marriage. My father was a kind, loving dad, who would have done anything for his children. My mom was very nurturing and loving, as well as selfless and giving. They were good together. I dreamt of one day having a marriage like theirs. Although my dad passed away when I was pretty young, he taught me many lessons, most of all, how to respect myself and how I should expect to be treated by other people. Most little girls believe they have the best father in the world. Well, I did.

Fast forward several years; I could never have imagined I would find myself in a psychologically, emotionally, and physically abusive marriage. At the time, it seemed as if the abuse had come out of nowhere. But if I'm being honest in my reflection, there were many signs of the person my partner really was. As I think back, the control and manipulation had started with certain behaviors. He would comment on my clothes, saying I was dressing inappropriately for work and I wore too much makeup. If I went anywhere without him, he wanted me to call whenever I reached my destination. At times, when I called as instructed, he would ask to speak to my friends, asking to say hi to them, obviously checking if I was where I said I was. He would call when I arrived at work and when I was leaving work. I thought it was his way of being concerned and making sure I was safe. At twenty-five, it was my first serious relationship, what did I know? My friends and family voiced their opinions to me. No one liked him. My mother didn't like him, but she couldn't put her finger on exactly why, other than he was disingenuous. I ignored everyone, even my own instincts.

After about six months of dating, we secretly got married because no one in my family would have approved or given us their blessings. Immediately after getting married, the abuse escalated to a whole new level. He started calling me horrible names. Each day he chipped away at my self-esteem. He assured me I wouldn't be going anywhere now that we were married. The physical abuse began shortly afterward. He was grabbing, pushing, punching, and choking. One evening after work, I didn't come straight home, and all hell broke loose. He accused me of cheating and refused to let me get in bed. When I went to lay down, he literally kicked me out of bed. This kind of thing went on for several years. I never knew what to expect when I got home. I didn't recognize myself while all of this was going on. I became a totally different person. I started thinking about all kinds of crazy things. I used to think of ways to kill him and how I could get away with it. I imagined suffocating him in his sleep, then cutting up his body in the tub, or throwing it in the incinerator. I felt so alone, so isolated from my friends and family. My world became small and dark. I spent a lot of time alone because I didn't want to have to explain the bruises. I didn't want to have to lie about why I didn't visit them anymore. I felt as if I was responsible for the situation I was in. There I was, a college graduate, pursuing my career in social work, counseling people on domestic violence and how to keep themselves safe, while I was living a textbook scenario of domestic violence. My spirit was broken, and I had no relationship with God. I thought he had forgotten about me. I couldn't understand the kind of marriage I found myself trapped in. When I became pregnant, I was so excited because I knew I wanted to be a mom. Unfortunately, my husband wasn't as excited; he said, "This is not our five-year plan."

He proceeded to threaten me and eventually pressured me into terminating the pregnancy. I didn't feel strong enough to fight, so I gave in. My self-esteem was at an all-time low. I was existing, but I wasn't living. Several months after the termination, I became pregnant again. His views and position remained the same as before. This time, I was determined not to terminate the pregnancy. Then, during a night of arguing, he said, "If you keep that baby, you may find yourself falling down some stairs and having a terrible accident." At that point, I was afraid for myself and my child. I began praying, "God, please help me get out of this hell safely." One day, shortly after I had started praying, He spoke to me in the shower, saying, "You are my child, and this is not what I want for you." At that very moment, I found I was no longer afraid. Everything became clear to me. I was no longer ashamed. Our next fight ended differently. I had the courage to call the police and have him removed from the house. I got an Order of Protection from the court. I had reconnected with God, and I felt His presence in my life once more. He gave me the strength I didn't know I had.

I went through my entire pregnancy on my own. I gave birth to my daughter and was comfortable being a single mom. Out of nowhere, my husband started to show some interest in our daughter. I began to feel guilty because I was not giving my brand-new baby a two-parent home like the one I had had. I let him return home and tried to make things work. He showed some love and concern towards our daughter. Although he was there, I was the primary caretaker; a breastfeeding mom with a full-time job, with little support from him. It felt like he was a roommate. What had I expected? He didn't want to have the baby in the first place. It wasn't long before the verbal and psychological abuse began, but I wasn't afraid this time. I was like a lioness protecting her cub. I was able to fight back. I knew this time I had God on my side. I abandoned the marriage with my daughter.

However, despite my fight-back, I didn't escape the relationship without bruises, and I was very bitter for a while. I found it hard to trust people. People saw me as "the angry black woman."

For years, I stayed angry at my husband. I blamed him for my hate. I blamed him for my having lost trust in people. While I was drowning in a pool of being bitter, he was living his best life. He went on to remarry and had two more children. Me? I was miserable and lonely, surrounded by a wall of anger, contemplating how I might get revenge for the time and pain he had cost me. Dating and socializing was the farthest thing from my mind. But while I kept on putting myself through all that misery, he didn't have a clue and wouldn't have cared less if he had. It got to the point where I had to ask myself how all the anger was serving me. I realized I had to get through the situation myself; I had to work through the pain to start living my best life.

So, I focused on my relationship with Jesus Christ. I returned to church, studied my bible, prayed, and meditated. God led me to forgiveness, forgiving my husband for all the pain and hurt I believed he had caused me. God had been faithful to me, and I knew he would not steer me wrong. However, I wasn't done yet. I had to forgive myself, too. I blamed myself for having chosen this man to be the father of my daughter. His absence caused her pain and, in turn, caused me pain. Forgiving was such a release, like a great weight being lifted off me. My perspective on life grew clearer, and I realized being angry and hating people clouded my judgment and robbed me of wonderful experiences. Being angry only created a negative energy around me, all the time. How can any good come to me in the presence of such anger? I finally managed to get over that wall and began to trust again. I asked God for healing, so I would not take the negative baggage into my next relationship. I prayed it would be with a man like my father.

Today, I am with my soulmate. He respects me and supports me. He honors me and treats me like a lady. He loves my children and me. We share common interests and dreams. I trust him and he trusts me. He wants the best for me and takes care of me like my father used to. I realize now that my dream as a little girl was actually God's preview for my life.

Over the years, as I have reflected on that awful period of my life, I realize it taught me three important things:

1. God will present you with opportunities to let go and forgive; you just have to be willing to do it or repeat the lesson. Not forgiving hurts you but never hurts the other person. Even more damage happens when you cannot forgive yourself.

2. Going through life not being able to forgive is a bit like driving with a rain-drenched windshield; you may be able to see, but everything is greatly distorted. Not being able to forgive creates a bitterness in your soul you may not realize exists. That bitterness blocks your ability to experience the fullness of life and the people in it. Your response to the world is from an angry perspective.

3. Forgiveness gave me an internal joy. It gave me peace so that now I can quickly forgive and ask for forgiveness. Holding grudges and being angry with people takes a lot of energy. I compare it to Post Traumatic Stress Disorder; you just have to think about the "offense," and you get as angry as if it has just happened when it might have been five years ago! I've learned forgiveness has brought me my own peace.

In the work that I do, many people dealing with addiction struggle with forgiveness of others and themselves. They struggle with releasing that pain and, therefore, self-medicate. I have no regrets about what I went through. I have my eldest daughter, who is now twenty-three and a college graduate. She is such a strong, wonderful, lovely young woman who is kind and loving. I praise God for who she is.

My experience with my ex-husband showed me the signs to avoid in potential partners once I began dating again. I am happy to say, I am now with my soulmate. Most importantly, I have reconnected with Jesus Christ. I believe if I had not gone through that terrible experience during my first marriage, my relationship with God would not be what it is today. If you find yourself struggling to forgive, know that there is power in forgiveness. You have nothing to lose but so much to gain. Be assured that joy, grace, mercy, and blessings await you on the other side of forgiveness.

## BIOGRAPHY

Stephanie Woodley is a resident of Harlem, New York. She's a certified addiction counselor, life coach, network marketer, and frequent traveler. Her undergraduate and graduate studies were at Hunter College. She received her addiction certification at Lehman College. She has counseled and coached at Mount Sinai Hospital Behavioral Center for over two decades. She is on two committees in 1199 SEIU, supporting her colleagues. She has hours of training on Motivational Interviewing and Informed Trauma training. She has helped thousands in their journey to recovery. Throughout her experiences as a counselor and coach, she realizes that many people struggle with a common issue; forgiveness. Having faced some challenges herself in that area, she is now sharing what she has learned to benefit others. Her passions are helping people live their best lives, spending time with her family, and traveling the world.

Connect with Stephanie Woodley via https://linktr.ee/Stephaniewoodley

CHAPTER 30

# Accounting For The Unknown

*By Tet Dela Cruz*

A few years ago, my family moved to Canada. Back home, my husband and I were in corporate management roles. Our son was studying in an exclusive school. We were able to build our investment portfolio, and I can say we were financially stable. There were many good reasons to stay. Yet, here we are, out of our comfort zones. You might be wondering what made me consider moving abroad. Here are some of my self-reflections.

**My Musts**

I worked the night shift, and my husband worked the day shift. We both work long hours. By the time he'd get home, I would be ready to leave for office. My body recuperated on weekends, and I slept for the most part of my Saturdays. We attended Mass on Sundays and did our groceries right after as the supermarket was just beside the church. We'd visit my mother as she lived nearby. There went my weekends. It got me thinking: Am I living the life I was meant to live? That question brought me to my first reflection. What are the things that matter to me most? My musts. My non-negotiables. My answers were clear to me: my God, my family, and my health. I would not compromise on these should we decide to relocate.

Spiritual: Will we be free to practice what we believe?

Family: Will we be able to spend quality time with our loved ones?

Health: Will we be able to care about ourselves physically and mentally?

If you are thinking of relocating, list down your musts. If you answered "No" to any of them, you might want to ask yourself, "Why not stay put?"

**Quality of Life**

My next reflections were on my hopes and dreams for myself and my loved ones. I thought about our careers, education, investments, sports, leisure, activities, and support groups. These are intangible things that would make our life enjoyable and meaningful. Quality of life is highly subjective as it pertains to one's perception of happiness. As ironic as it may sound, the accountant in me associates a cost and perceived value to all of these.

I did much research for the list below. The cost was based on what I anticipated to earn and spend in Canada. The perceived value was the price I was willing to pay for each of the factors below.

*Career*: This was the easiest part for me, as there are plenty of sources available online. There was also a Job Bank embedded within the Government of Canada website. I used the average salary for our profession.

*Health*: This is where both the cost and perceived value came into play. The cost was for the premium of private health insurance for services not covered by the provincial health coverage. The perceived value was for the price I would have to pay for the services. To put it in context, if you went to the dentist twice a year for a specific dental work, you would include the amount you would have paid, assuming you did not have health insurance.

*Education*: I checked both the public and private institutions. I spent a considerable amount of time here because our house selection would also depend on our child's school. I will not get into great detail here, but some things to consider are attendance areas or school eligibility, school bus eligibility, and school ranking. Generally, children can only go to the school located in the attendance area where they reside. Our international driver's license was only valid for a few months. Therefore, identifying walk zones and bused areas was essential for us. Just as with health, I considered both the cost and perceived value.

*Savings and Investments*: I must admit that I did not put much thought into the details here. I allocated a certain percentage for savings and investments, and that was it. Determining the disposable income was a prerequisite, as it was the basis for identifying the percentage.

*Leisure and Other Activities*: My family shares a passion for travel. So, knowing the average cost of a vacation was on top of our list. I included at least one activity per season. I also included sports in this section. My son was into fencing, which I figured was less popular than other sports. Fortunately, there was a fencing club near one of the schools we were considering.

*Support Group*: I do not think this is something we can put a price on as it is more about relationships. I did not want to leave it out, as it was essential for our well-being. For the cost, I looked for professional and social organizations and checked the membership fees. I factored in the possible expenses to be incurred when attending the meetings or social gatherings.

Quality of life varies according to your personal preferences. Later in this chapter, I will explain how I used cost versus perceived value and how we used it in making the most informed decision possible.

**Cost of Living**

My definition of cost of living may be different from how an economist would define it. My focus was on what my typical day looked like. Unlike quality of life, the factors I listed here were not based on my preferences, but rather, necessities.

The question I had was: "Am I ready to let go of what I was accustomed to and embrace new cultures, traditions, and ways of life?"

Here are the things I considered. Needless to say, I also associated costs to each of them.

*Shelter*: After we identified the top three schools for my child, we began to look for a place to live. It had to be strategic as I anticipated commuting as we settled in. I considered the proximity to the grocery store, church, school, and work. Believe it or not, I checked it down to the bus number I needed to ride going to work. For calculation purposes, I added the insurance, utilities, and all other accommodation expenses.

*Taxes*: Spending rates would depend on our disposal income, and taxes would be key in identifying it.

*Transportation*: Commuting expenses were different for the first year. It would eventually be replaced with the actual costs of owning a vehicle. I included all transportation-related expenses such as bus fare, fuel, insurance, and amortization. This included going to work, sports/recreational facilities, school, and wherever we wanted to be.

*Climate*: We were coming from a tropical country. The climate would affect our clothing, utilities, and health.

*Food*: I am a picky eater. I researched the price of the foods I typically eat and how to get to the store.

*Others*: Banks, and yes, shopping!

The simple and familiar comforts that I took for granted were what I missed most during our first few months. I did not realize that the thickness of a pasta noodle would matter to me until we cooked spaghetti for the first time in our new home. I am glad that I considered the cost of living as it helped me adjust and have the proper and global mindset.

**Changes/Adjustments**

It was my husband who wanted to live abroad. It so happened that I was the one who was given the opportunity to relocate abroad. My family supported me from the beginning, but I was the one who needed convincing.

Now, for the adjustments, it was really a matter of how significantly living abroad would affect our musts, quality of life, and cost of living.

For a basis of comparison, I compared each section I listed above against what we had back home.

*Musts*: Would it change for the better? And was it really worth the one-way ticket? Yes, for sure, you can easily book a ticket back home if it will not work out for you and your family. I bet you would not want that. I have mentioned earlier that if you answered "No" to any of your "must" questions, then, maybe, you should reflect on staying put. I honestly think that I cannot ignore red flags. It would not make sense to move forward having assessed the changes to our quality of life and cost of living if we were not able to satisfy all of our "musts," with the emphasis on "all." Having said this, it is vital that only the top things you can live without should make it to the list.

*Quality of Life*: For the cost, I calculated our opportunity losses and gains. Having a perceived value made it a bit easier to compare, as it was quantified. I had also factored in some downsides for moving, like starting over. Creating a fresh start scared me the most. On the other hand, I considered perks like studying or working abroad being very attractive to employers should we decide to go back home.

*Cost of Living*: Similar to quality of life, I identified the opportunity cost and gains. I analyzed each of the items I had under cost of living. I briefly touched on disposable income under my 'taxes' factor. On this note, I included the purchasing power, like how quickly we'd be able to achieve our financial goals.

Important decisions, especially those that were life-changing, required us to gather as much information as possible, identify all potential alternatives we could think of, and measure every conceivable outcome from all possible angles. I know that not everything can be quantified and measured. It is helpful to ask those who have been in the same situation. Sometimes, you should also trust your intuition.

When you find yourself overwhelmed by too many thoughts swirling around in your head, take a step back. Reflect on where your deep 'Why' is moving. Make sure you are not evading a temporary situation or challenge. Remember that moving abroad is a long-term, life-changing event, and you should be doing it for the right reasons.

Maybe it is too early to say this, but moving to Canada was one of the best decisions I made for my family and me.

> *"Only those who will risk going too far can possibly find out how far one can go."*[25]
> —T.S. Eliot

## BIOGRAPHY

Tet Dela Cruz is a Filipino Certified Public Accountant based in Canada. With a background in corporate leadership, her career expands over information technology, finance, and audit industries. She worked her way up from rank and file to a senior management role. Fuelled by not living a life she was meant to be and the feeling of existing but not living, she pushed herself out of her comfort zone and boldly relocated to a country she had never been to. She is passionate about helping people leverage their focus on what matters most at work and their personal lives and reach new heights. Capitalizing on her accounting and leadership experiences, she seamlessly transitioned to a different country. She is a member of the Philippine Institute of Certified Public Accountants (PICPA) and the Association of Filipino Canadian Accountants (AFCA). She is a part-time entrepreneur. Tet enjoys traveling and spending quality time with her family. She currently resides in Ontario with her husband and son.

Connect with Tet Dela Cruz via https://linktr.ee/tetdelacruz

---

25 "T. S. Eliot Quotes," BrainyQuote (Xplore), accessed May 24, 2021 https://www.brainyquote.com/quotes/t_s_eliot_161678.

CHAPTER 31

# Tragic Blessings

*By Todd and Gina Strand*

Sometimes the worst and best things happen to us at exactly the same moment. Today, it sucks! Down the road, you'll look back and realize that the "tragic event" ended up sowing the seeds of new beginnings that would serve you and bless others. Make no mistake, one cannot achieve the crown without the cross, and the promised land almost always lies on the other side of a journey through the wilderness. The cross is different for each of us, and all who enter the promised land are first tested in the harshness of the desert. How we embrace our journey determines two things: Will we get into the promised land? How long will our journey take?

Here's our journey. We hope it serves and inspires you and that your "test" will serve as a "<u>TEST</u>imony" for the generation that follows you.

The Promised Land

As we type, we are the top income earners in our company, and our team has spread to sixty-three countries and growing. Our income seems to go up effortlessly as we travel the world, helping our team grow. Our biggest goal today is to leave a legacy of helping others succeed and spending time with our family.

We feel like we are part of a fairytale, and the promise is well worth the price, but there were countless times of fear, economic hardship, struggle, shattered dreams, doubt, and feeling like a sacrifice on someone's altar.

Welcome to the Wilderness (Todd)

I grew up in Champaign, IL, where my parents provided for me, my brother, and my sister. My mother and father were hard workers; they both worked multiple jobs in addition to their primary jobs as city bus driver and policeman, respectively. They sent us kids to a private school (St. Matthew's), where I learned I was the poor, fat kid. We weren't really poor, but compared to the rich kids at St. Matthew's, it felt that way. These years were some of the hardest of my youth as I was relentlessly picked on for being overweight and poor. The most popular kid in my class told me point-blank: "You will never win." I was devastated. However, this pain was my blessing. A seed was planted in me, and I was determined to be something more than average.

My big break came when I was thirteen. My father helped me kickstart a thriving lawn care business. In high school, I was a rich little kid (hamburgers for everyone) with classmates who worked for me. A year after graduating high school in 1989, I borrowed $100,000, and I grew my lawn care company to be the biggest in the Champaign county, with ten trucks on the road and twenty-five employees at our peak. However, the bigger we got and the harder I worked, the less we made. I was frustrated! I began to subscribe to Forbes and other magazines. I found out about a company called Nightingale Conant that sold audios on success. I began to read and listen to everything I could, still so determined to become something more than average. The pain of struggle set me on a lifelong path of continuous learning and personal development—a huge blessing.

In 1994, at the age of twenty-three, my accountant invited me to learn about the Direct Selling Industry. The gentleman giving the presentation earned $60,000 per month with no employees, no bookkeeping, no accounts receivable, no warehouses, no mechanics, no inventory, and no capital expenditure. I was drooling all over myself.

I enthusiastically decided to give up the company I had built for ten years and pursue network marketing full-time from day one. It's as if I was auditioning to star in the movie *Dumb and Dumber*. Going full-time into an industry you know nothing about is a horrible idea, but I was twenty-three and enthusiastic. I worked hard, but I did not have the slightest idea on how to build the business, and I ultimately went flat broke.

Later that year, my mother died of pancreatic cancer on my twenty-fourth birthday. She was only forty-nine. The tragedy of that moment was overwhelming, but it also carried with it the ultimate lesson: Life is short, and you better live it now.

I was broke and broken-hearted, but I was now more determined than ever to not waste my life in a cubicle building someone else's dream. I dug in further; however, my fiancé couldn't understand my passion and decided to dump me since I was now a financial wreck.

Luckily, I had recruited a few students at the University of Illinois into my networking venture, and they allowed me to sleep on a futon in the basement of the townhouse they rented. I had no bank account, no money, no food, no home, and no car during this time. If it weren't for Pascal, Tom, and Serge believing in me and the networking business we were pursuing, I would be out in the cold.

They allowed me to use their phone, and I smiled and dialed and dialed and dialed and dialed and dialed and dialed, determined that there had to be a way to make this venture work, but I continued to just spin my wheels. Looking back today, I realized I was forming work habits in the crucible of "the networking desert." I was developing prospecting habits. I learned that you need to say less to more people. What seemed like more pain was really more blessings. Ultimately, I was willing to do it wrong enough and long enough—for two years—until I had a breakthrough.

After two years of success in our industry, the company I was with fell on hard times (1997) and faced the possibility of going out of business.

I went running that summer, and I heard an audiotape from several tax professionals talking about all the tax advantages of a home-based business. In 1997, most people mentioned the tax advantages, but nobody really knew what they were or how to legally take them. So, I helped the company recruit a dream team of tax experts, including Sandy Botkin. We put together a program helping average people understand home business tax savings permitted by the law. The company exploded in growth. Our sales reached $100 million in two and a half years. We were featured in books, and many of the experts in our space thought we were the next giant. We couldn't brag about ourselves enough!

I met my wife Gina and some of my dearest friends in that company. However, in the fall of 2000, the regulatory bodies attacked the company viscously, causing the company's demise and landing me in legal jeopardy. I will never forget the moment that an attorney told me that I could end up in prison for my involvement in a company where I took pride. The challenge was the company grew so fast they didn't hire the attorneys to dot the i's and cross the t's. I ultimately had to fall on my sword (one of the hardest days of my life) and take a plea deal. That meant I would have to serve forty months in prison. There I was: a guy who always looked for companies with credibility; a guy who would give money back to the cashier when they gave me too much change. And now, I AM GOING TO PRISON?! ARE YOU @#$%ING KIDDING ME?! Welcome to the wilderness! Although there is a 99.9% chance none of you will have this type of *wilderness* experience, it doesn't make the one you might have any easier. In my shock and grief over what seemed like such an undeserved predicament, I began to feel sorry for myself and threw one of the world's best pity parties. However, a week into my pity party, I got a call to help coach the girls' softball team. I was being asked because the coach I was replacing (Mark) just learned that he had leukemia. I fell back in my chair. We knew Mark and his family. He neither smoked nor drank. He was a super nice guy that worked as a butcher and raised a great family. He was in his forties, just like my mom, and he was faced with life and death. I realized at that moment, no matter how bad you think you have it, someone will always be ready to switch places with you in a heartbeat.

So, instead of complaining about my predicament, I decided to embrace it. I began to ask myself: How could I make the next forty months in prison some of the best months of my life? It was a daily mental struggle with a full set of emotions, ranging from anger to disbelief, but perhaps this was the opportunity. This was the test. My wife and I kept reminding ourselves that we couldn't control what happened to us; all we could do was control our response. We could choose faith or fear, positive or negative, blessings or curses. It really is a choice.

Welcome to the desert. I checked myself in at the prison camp in Tucson, AZ, believing that I would make the best of my situation, but I could never have imagined how the experience would transform me, my wife, and our life.

Blessings of the Desert:

- I came across the most amazing people (doctors, lawyers, bankers, and one congressman); many are still dear friends with my wife and me today.
- I lost fifty-two pounds and got into the best shape of my life.
- I got to read seventy-five books per year.
- I grew closer to my wife, Gina, than I had ever been. Her faith still inspires me.
- My relationship with the Lord grew in indescribable ways, and I learned that you never really know that all you need is God until all you have is God.
- I was able to study the Bible in the same place most of it was written—prison!
- I discovered I could teach people everything they needed to know to build a geometrically growing network marketing organization straight out of the Bible.
- I taught a class every Friday called "Biblical Secrets of Network Marketing" to a "captive" audience at the prison.
- I passionately committed myself to this incredible industry called Network Marketing.

After the forty-month journey in the desert, everything seemed smaller and easier. We had a renewed sense of passion and purpose. My wife enrolled us in a new networking company, and we began to build. Our team started small, but then it began to blossom. We were having the time of our lives, and six months into our campaign, we received news that my wife Gina had cervical cancer. Gina was forty-eight. At that age, my mom received the diagnosis of her cancer. I was scared, and I thought: How much struggle and testing does one have to take? Again, Gina displayed the most amazing faith and stated that all things happen in God's time. We embraced the Scripture that taught to give thanks in all circumstances. We weren't thankful for cancer, but we were grateful for the doctors who performed the three surgeries. We were grateful for the chemo and radiation that made her cancer-free. We were thankful to have residual income, insurance, and the love and support of our family and friends. We kept building our business through the process, and our team continued to grow.

Over time our team spread to sixty-three countries, and we became the top income earners in the company. We unequivocally would not be enjoying the blessings of today without all of the struggles along the way. We've learned that the setbacks are setups for something bigger and that with every adversity comes the seeds of equal and greater blessings.

Everyone's journey to the Promised Land is unique. We are all tested in different ways along the way. How we respond and handle our tests or challenges will determine whether we enter our Promised Land just as it did for the Israelites escaping Egypt in the book of Genesis. This is the story of life! We pray that you find your blessings and enjoy your Promised Land.

"Now listen! Today I am giving you a choice between life and death, between prosperity and disaster . . . between blessings and curses. Now I call on heaven and earth to witness the choice you make" (Deuteronomy 30:15, 19 NLT).

# BIOGRAPHY

Todd and Gina Strand have been top income earners in the direct selling industry for over two decades. Their team has spread to sixty-three countries, and they teach a course called "Biblical Secrets of Network Marketing" all around the world. Todd and Gina are true servant leaders who teach and inspire others to reach their full potential, working from the comfort of their homes.

Connect with Todd and Gina Strand via https://linktr.ee/ToddandGina

CHAPTER 32

# Everyone Can Be A Winner

*By Wincy Chan*

Have you ever felt like you are a loser? I have. There are obstacles and difficulties in life which make us feel like losers: not nailing that perfect job; not marrying that perfect guy or girl; not getting into that perfect university; not grabbing that perfect project; and many others. For me, it was not getting a good enough grade that would get me into "that perfect senior high school."

    I still remember the day I received the results of my standardized exam (something like an ACT or SAT), for which I needed good grades in order to get into "my perfect senior high school" and "my perfect college" later on. While many of my classmates rejoiced and celebrated their successes, I was shocked, and it caught me by surprise that I was kicked out of the game.

    I was never the brightest student in class, but I was not a "bottomer" either. I was expected to join my friends in senior high school. Instead, I was derailed. In Asian countries, high academic results were considered an incredible feat (and they still are), and not getting good grades or getting into college almost meant it was a disgrace to the family. This was especially true for me because I was the eldest child in the family. I would have been the first college graduate in the entire clan. My plan got whacked, and my world turned upside down. It was the first time in my life that I felt like I was a loser.

**Born a Loser? Or Made a Loser?**

If you ask a random person, "What's the purpose of education?" I bet the most common answers you would get are "to educate," "to develop," or "to prepare children for a better future." However, being a primary, high school, and college teacher (I'll share more on my background later) for more than fourteen years, as well as a traditional student for more than twenty-three years, I can tell you that the purpose of modern education is to NEITHER prepare children for a better future NOR develop them to become more confident adults. Instead, the modern education system trains and produces workers, soldiers, and followers. It emphasizes conformity over creativity, values answers over questions, and embraces followers over leaders. In the process, this "one size fits all" system uses one barrier after another in trying to sieve out all those who "do not fit in." To achieve this goal, the system creates this thing called "exams," as a result of which people who are "not born with it" would eventually be kicked out of the system. As a result, many "losers" were left on the street, and the system was left with "non-losers" who survived the barriers. However, the sad truth is that they were not necessarily "winners." They were people who had "made the fewest mistakes," and they had their own battle within the system. It's like having a tree-climbing contest in the forest. All animals would have to participate: elephants, giraffes, lions, sharks, and monkeys. Of course, everyone lost except the monkeys, and everyone was sent away from the forest because they were not monkeys. Instead, imagine if we had a weightlifting contest for the elephants, a leaf-eating from tall trees contest for the giraffes, a hunting contest for the lions, a swimming contest for the sharks. Everyone would be champions, and everyone would be able to perform their best. That should be the purpose of education. Education should nurture winners, not make losers.

**The Turning Point**

I was not aware that "I am a loser" was a lie until I had the opportunity to explore the world. I lived with this tattoo on my forehead for a long time, and I tried to do anything to prove to anyone that I was not a loser, I was not a failure, and I was not a disgrace to my family. After failing my first attempt at the standardized exam, I studied for one more year and failed again. While I was supposed to find a job or help with my family business, a little fish shop in the wet market, I was offered a chance to study abroad in the United States. I was skeptical about my ability and felt uneasy about leaving all my friends and family behind and studying in a place where I had never been. Yet, I was grateful that I had a chance to prove that I was not a loser. Time flew. Five years had passed, and I had finished my Bachelor of Arts in Fine Art. During my college life, my horizons were widened. I was exposed to a whole new way of learning, where questions and differences were welcomed, where teachers could be challenged, where faults and mistakes were allowed, and students were eager to learn. For the first time, I felt that learning could be an enjoyable experience. I didn't want anyone to go through what I had been through; instead, I wanted to create a learning environment where children could really enjoy learning. So, I became a primary and secondary school teacher after returning to Hong Kong.

**The Second Turning Point**

I worked in an elite school. It consisted of grades one through twelve. I had a chance to teach students from all grades throughout my eight years of teaching in that school, given my specific skill set and background.

Being part of the system, it didn't take much time to realize that I had become one of the accomplices who helped hand out "I am a loser" stickers. The founding principal had a good heart to start the school with a focus on a humanistic approach with minimal exams and a low emphasis on grades. As time passed, the principal faced increasing pressure from parents and the school board, which demanded higher academic results. Eventually, exams and grades became the end goal of learning instead of learning how to think and how to solve problems. For me, teaching had become a job rather than a mission. Even though I didn't feel right, life was too comfortable that I did not have the urge to change.

During the hot summer of 2012, my first child was born. Maybe it was parental instinct, but even though the baby was still a few days old, I was already thinking about his future, his future career, future wife, future family, etc. And inevitably, I thought about his education. I've seen so many children going into Grade I with sparks in their eyes throughout my teaching career, full of excitement and curiosity. As time went on, their sparks got smaller and smaller, and they became teenagers who had no interest in anything. They might live till their eighties, but their hearts died at fifteen. I told myself I couldn't let that happen to my child.

In the coming years, I actively looked for alternative approaches to educate my kids. I had another child two years after my firstborn. I believed there must be a way in which kids can learn enjoyably and purposely. In pursuit of this kind of education, I left my full-time teaching job and homeschooled my children for five and a half years. Through the journey, I was able to look into different education systems. Finally, I decided to put my children in an alternative education program, an education system that was truly child-centered. Its curriculum was designed based on the physical, psychological, and emotional development of children. I had also become a teacher in that alternative education system trying to bring quality education to society and nurture children "the right way."

I would like to share the three important lessons that I learned on this journey of questing for suitable education.

1. Listen to Your Heart

    God does not create clones. Throughout the history of humankind, there has never been a single person like YOU. It has never been the case, and it never will be. You are shaped in such a way that only you can achieve what you are made of. During my time at the university, Business was the hottest subject of all. Everybody went to business school; I was no exception. My parents had high hopes for me (being the first college student in the clan); they expected me to be one of those "high street bankers" and bring glory to the family. After one semester of "torture," I knew in my heart that I was built for something more practical, more hands-on. I then bravely switched to Fine Art despite massive opposition from my parents. Even though I felt sorry that my parents were worried, sad, and disappointed, when I look back on my journey, studying art truly enlightened me, and that was the first time I could "enjoy" learning. And because I really enjoyed learning art, I thrived in it, which enabled me to develop a career.

2. Live on Your Purpose

Two forces that drive people's decisions: one is faith, and the other one is fear. If a person decides based on fear, what he focuses on are the disadvantages of the current situation. His primary focus will be to escape what is happening or what will happen to him or his family if he doesn't take action. However, actions based on fear are usually quick, which means the chances of heading into another disadvantageous situation are high because he does not have enough time to research, digest, and listen to his heart. On the contrary, a person who makes decisions based on faith focuses on where he wants to go and what he wants to achieve in the future. He would not be limited by his current situations, resources, or abilities. Instead, he would look for resources and develop abilities to achieve desirable situations or outcomes. Faith is believing in something that hasn't happened yet. Even though my kids are only nine and six right now, I have strong faith that their future will be bright as ever because what I am adopting is a humanistic education system that has proven itself for over 100 years; I spent time researching it and witnessing the results myself. Knowing what you want is more important than knowing what you don't want at the end of the day.

3. Commit to Lifelong Learning

One thing that helped me fight the "I am a loser" feeling and let me accomplish whatever I have was my lifelong learning commitment. I never quit learning. It kept me flexible in adapting to different situations and circumstances. From never-left-home to studying abroad alone in a foreign country, from a mainstream teacher to an alternative educator, from a hands-on person to a writing person, I had been through so many changes in my life. More changes are inbound, and I know I am ready because I am committed to lifelong learning.

My elder son is a bright, smart, and eager-to-learn Grade II student, and my younger daughter is a cheerful, helpful, and full-of-curiosity kindergarten student. I know that I had made the right choices for them, and I hope that my perseverance in questing for an education that "truly educates" children, will encourage those in doubt about education or doubt that learning can be practical and enjoyable at the same time. I believe that **no one is a loser**. Instead, **everyone can be a winner**.

## BIOGRAPHY

Wincy Chan is a "teacherpreneur" and an alternative educator who is passionate about child development, school education, and parenting. She was interviewed by mass media on TV and published newspaper articles, sharing her unique views on educating children with humanistic approaches and art. Her teaching experiences in both mainstream education and alternative education made her unique in understanding the advantages and disadvantages of both systems. Her mission is to bring alternative education to public awareness while helping mainstream education move toward a more children-centred approach—physically, psychologically, and emotionally—in teaching. Eventually, all children can be nurtured "the right way."

Connect with Wincy Chan via https://linktr.ee/WincyInspiration

The End

Manufactured by Amazon.ca
Bolton, ON